TORMENTED: 8 YEARS AND BACK

PEGGY JOYCE RUTH

Foreword: Frank D. Hammond

Printed in the United States of America

Impact Christian Books, Inc.
332 Leffingwell Ave.
Kirkwood, MO 63122
314 822 3309
www.impactchrisianbooks.com

My sincere appreciation to:
Marcus Stallworth of Dallas, Texas, for the cover design
Carolyn Brandenburg, Lloyd Ford, Janice Toyne for editing
Pastor Jimmy and Lynda Low for theology confirmation
Angelia Schum for manuscript layout

ISBN 0 89228-177-4

Table of Contents

ACKNOWLEDGEMENTS

I dedicate this book in sincere appreciation to my husband, Jack, for his undying love and care during the long years of sickness when there was no end in sight and no light at the end of the tunnel. He has been the love of my life for forty-four wonderful years. Words could never adequately express the love and gratitude I feel for his untiring, faithful support.

...And to my mother, Peggy Crow, who not only poured herself into me in my growing up years, but also continued to care for me physically and emotionally through those dark years in my early adult life. No one would be able to count the hours she so unselfishly sowed into my life and into the lives of my children at a time when I so desperately needed her.

Foreword

Here is a testimony that will not only hold your attention but will also captivate your heart! Descend with Peggy Joyce Ruth to the depths of despair and desperation, and ascend with her to the heights of joyous victory. Come away with a fresh appreciation for the Word of God and its rewards to those who believe. Discover the truth that deliverance is not an event, but a process in spiritual growth. Learn for yourself how to fill the empty places after evil spirits have been cast out. This book is a faith-builder for all whose hope is lost or deferred. You will be blessed with spiritual enlightenment and encouragement.

Frank D. Hammond, Author
Pigs in the Parlor

Foreword

There are many books about deliverance, but the thing that sets this book apart is the emphasis on maintaining deliverance. Many people receive deliverance, but fail to fill their house with the Word of God as the scripture admonishes. (Matthew 12: 43-45) Peggy Joyce fought an intense battle between faith and fear. She utterly purged her thought life of negative assaults from the devil. No other book I have read on deliverance—and I have read most of them—gives such positive, workable steps on how to overcome the battle that takes place in the mind. This book contains some of the best material I have found on the thought life.

Jimmy Low
Pastor in Plainview & Muleshoe, TX, for 37 years

Introduction

Like no other time in history, people seem to be more fascinated with the supernaturally evil, dark side of life. More movies and books dealing with witchcraft, new age, sorcery... have been produced in this decade than ever before. The world dabbles in the occult as though it were some parlor game, totally oblivious to the danger that lies within. Interestingly, what people do not realize is that there is truly an evil force in the world that is not allegorical. Throughout the Bible, beginning with Genesis and ending with Revelation, it speaks extensively about evil and its source. However, we as Christians often shy away from the subject. We state that we believe in the Bible but distance ourselves from accepting the fact that *Satan and his evil spirits roam about this world seeking those he can devour* (I Peter 5: 8).

Christ spent much of His earthly ministry taking authority over Satan, and He was very candid about the troubles one can encounter as a result of the evil rulers and forces in the heavenlies. However, despite everything that has been stated in the Scriptures about the evil spirits that are against us, for the most part, Christians for years have buried their head in the sand. But when Frank Hammonds wrote *Pigs in the Parlor,* a very modern mindset to the reality of demonic spirits was exposed.

Over 30 years ago my mother suffered from Clinical Chronic Neurosis. At the time she diligently sought the natural means of healing, but unfortunately, medical doctors and psychiatrists could offer no permanent help. Practically every known type of medication and source of treatment was administered without success. Interestingly, the key to her healing was not a *hidden* truth found in the Bible, but one candidly spoken about by Christ. Mother finally had no alternative but to consider the fact that the demons and demonic forces referred to in the Scriptures might be the reason for her condition. The basis of her search was founded upon the belief that if God was *the same yesterday, today and forever*, the evil in this world was also the same yesterday, today and forever; therefore, Satan was still roaming about this world seeking those he could kill, steal and destroy (John 10:10).

We are living in a time when it is the norm to take Valium as a means of overcoming the anxieties of life. We are also living in a day when, despite how civilized our world has become, evil is alive and well in the hearts and souls of evil men. Evil will always war against good and against God. Even before 9/11, our country had spent billions of dollars to fight against evil. However, the Bible is clear that we cannot fight against a spiritual enemy with physical weapons.

My mother's road to recovery was not an easy journey. It was actually burdened by those of our own faith who discouraged her from considering the fact that demonic forces were destroying her life. Never have I seen a book like *TORMENTED: Eight Years and Back* that so adequately describes this type of problem and then so comprehensively and simplistically spells out the steps leading to a totally complete and victorious answer. For over 30 years my mother has continued to enjoy the divine mental and physical health that only God can provide.

William Wesley Ruth

Setting the Scene

Dr. Edgar Ezell, a psychiatrist practicing in Fort Worth, Texas, in 1970, after administering a series of electrical shock treatments, uttered the dreaded medical prognosis to my precious young, devastated husband, *"I don't know if I can guarantee that your wife will not have to be institutionalized. She will be on some form of anti-depressant the rest of her life. We don't know exactly what triggers these kinds of things. She might be fine one moment and completely lose it the next. I can only treat the symptoms—I cannot treat the cause because medical science does not know the cause of mental and emotional sickness."*

What on earth could have brought on this tragedy? Until this emotional devastation occurred, life had been wonderful. Jack and I had two and a half delightful years of blissful marriage, our precious little baby girl had just been born six months before and the future could not have looked brighter—when suddenly our entire world fell apart. How could this have happened? Could it have been avoided? Are there some clues that could save someone else from taking this detour through a living hell?

Chapter 1

PART I: MY TESTIMONY
Eight Years of Torment !

No one could have had a more ideal childhood. The oldest of three siblings, I was reared in a Christian home with wonderful parents who loved each other, loved us, and most of all, loved God. We were found in our little Baptist church practically every time the doors were open, surrounded by people who loved and supported us both spiritually and emotionally. I have great memories of summer camps, family vacations and a home open to all my fun-loving, noisy friends.

Later, I fell in love and married a wonderful, hard-working man who treated me like a queen. Two and a half years into the marriage, we started our family, and just six months after our first child was born in 1962, a Buddhist girl moved into the apartment behind us. Obligation, more than the leading of the Lord, motivated me to go to her apartment and attempt to share Jesus with her. Being reared in a Baptist church, I had a great many good foundational truths about salvation, but I had never been taught about spiritual warfare. This little Buddhist woman kept her house dark, constantly burned weird smelling incense and stayed to herself. All of those things made it hard to override my fear and make myself knock on her door. After I told her why I had come, she simply said that she expected to be given equal time.

I had no idea what I was getting into, nor did I remember one thing that I told her. I only remember that I had finished in just a few moments, and she began to tell me about her religion. The only thing that I honestly remember hearing from her was that I needed to keep an open mind. I have often said that I kept such an open mind that my brain fell out and I didn't find it until some eight years later. Nothing else that she said penetrated my conscious psyche, but while she was talking, my mind started reeling so hard and fast that I became confused and disoriented. (Before it was over I was going to feel that I could relate personally to Nebuchadnezzar in the book of Daniel, as he took on the mind of a beast for seven years of his life.)

My only conscious thought was to escape from this oriental woman's apartment as quickly as I could. With absolutely no physical restraints on me, I felt as helpless as a prisoner. My throat started constricting until I felt a choking sensation and doubts of all kinds began to bombard my mind. The rest of the afternoon I walked the streets around our apartment, desperately trying to pull my thinking back to normal. All of a sudden these *"what if"* thoughts started coming—*what if there is no God! What if the God I serve is not the right one! What if Jesus is not real!* I was totally panicked, but too ashamed of what was going on in my mind to tell anyone.

After Jack and I married, I joined the Methodist church with him. Out of desperation I finally made an appointment with our pastor—hoping that he could say something to me that would alleviate the torment I was in. On that first visit I knew my desperation was draining him emotionally, but I couldn't help myself. *I was* *desperate,* and he appeared to be my only hope. I had already sought help from the Brownwood medical community who thought I just needed to keep my mind occupied and everything would in time get back to normal.

One week after that first pastoral visit, I felt compelled to go back to see the pastor again, hoping against hope that maybe he had forgotten something helpful on the first visit that he would remember to tell me this time. After telling the pastor that I was in the waiting room, his secretary came back, apologetically saying that she didn't realize that he had already gone home for the day.

Sitting in my car in an almost hysterical state, trying to decide what to do next, I saw the pastor slip out the side door of the church, look cautiously in both directions, then make a dash for his car. Bless his heart! I realize now that he couldn't bring himself to face me again after what I had put him through the first time, but at the time I was devastated that his secretary had lied to me while he sneaked out a back way.

Upon realizing that even the pastor had no answers for me, I started having panic attacks regularly. Each new day was faced with a terrifying dread—but facing the night was no better. I constantly had to fight the urge to leave the house and just run as hard and fast as I could in an attempt to get away from the torment in my head. It was almost a paradox, because in spite of the urge to run, I felt so immobile that I could scarcely move. I found myself sitting for hours, just staring into space.

Finally, I entered a mental agony that I can't even begin to describe. All I wanted to do was escape into sleep. However, I would sleep so fitfully tormented by such terrifying nightmares that I found myself unable to quit convulsively crying practically every waking moment and even in my sleep. I had attempted to do my Christian duty and witness to someone about Jesus, without realizing that I had gone into a very intense spiritual battle with no armor on. And rather than affecting the Buddhist lady with what I had to say—she had, in fact, affected me. All my good intentions had only opened me up to spiritual warfare for which I was not prepared or trained.

I had long since quit praying or even opening my Bible because I was tormented the whole time with thoughts of *what if this is all just a joke*! I knew if I didn't do something I would die—so in my anguish, I came up with a plan. It wasn't a spiritual plan, but it was a mental plan to work my way out of my dilemma. As soon as Jack would leave for work I would go to the public library and read everything I could get my hands on about every foreign religion I could think of—trying to disprove *them* in an attempt to prove that Christianity was the right one.

These secret visits to the library went on for several months as I worked my way through every major religion: Islam, Buddhism, Hinduism and right on down through every minor religion that I had ever heard of. I recognized it as compulsive behavior, but I couldn't seem to help myself. When I would find something that convinced me that a certain religion was false, it would bring relief, but I would still mull over the findings for days, memorizing and reciting the convincing statement over and over. When, at last, I felt freed from the fear of that particular religion being right, I would feel compelled to just move on to my next investigation. I couldn't believe how many different religious sects came to my mind that I had never even consciously thought of before.

In that driven, tormented state, I must have stuck out like a sore thumb because the librarian found out who I was, called my husband and reported to him that she was concerned that something was wrong with me. After that, I was forbidden to go to the library and the entire extended family was alerted to keep a close eye on me. By this time I had slipped into such a compulsive behavior that I was driven to take encyclopedias out of my parent's house—concealed in the diaper bag or under my coat or in a sack—anyway to get them to my house so I could continue in my search to find what these different religions believed.

Finally the oppression became so bad that I was unable to stay by myself, so each morning on his way to work, Jack would leave me and our daughter at my mother's house. My mother began a regimen of things the world tells you to do to keep out of depression. The moment I arrived at her house she would open all the curtains, making the house as bright and cheery as possible. Every light in the house was turned on. Every project you can imagine—from planting flowers to baking and carrying food to the elderly—was put into practice. Mother took us on long drives in the country and for long walks in the neighborhood while attempting to engage me in conversation. She tried everything she could think of, but the stress that I realized I was putting on her, while at the same time feeling helpless to do anything about it, only plunged me more deeply into despair.

I would try to console myself with the fact that I had never had a prior history of this kind of behavior. I had been very successful in high school and college and had, in fact, been quite popular and surrounded by healthy relationships. So I tried to convince myself that with my emotionally stable background, surely this horrible nightmare would soon pass.

After weeks, however, of being carefully watched and only getting worse, Jack decided to take me to a psychiatrist. Thankfully, he found a Christian man—a Dr. Edgar Ezell, who, at the time, was the psychiatrist who screened many of the Baptist missionaries before they went overseas for a tour of duty. I remember the relief I felt when I thought—*"Now, hopefully, I will finally get some help!"* After hours of dialogue with me, Dr. Ezell decided to start a series of electrical shock treatments which lasted over a period of several months. Being taken into a back room, strapped down to a table as I watched the nurse apply the tourniquet before injecting my veins with intravenous medication to anesthetize me and knowing that the room would immediately begin spinning before I lost consciousness was something that I came to dread unmercifully. But I would have agreed to anything at that point, just to get some relief.

The shock therapy did seem to help temporarily because it would blank out my short term memory for a period of time. I have read that it actually kills brain cells. For a while I wouldn't be able to remember what I had been agonizing over, but even then, I was tormented with the knowledge that there was something bothering me badly enough to need help of such a drastic measure. It was like everything seemed OK in the front of my mind, but in the back of my mind the torment was still there.

After the months of shock treatments, I was put on anti-depressants that I was told would be needed for the rest of my life. The drugged feeling kept me wanting to sleep practically all day—partially from feeling drugged and partially because I was miserable when I was awake.

The shock therapy was only a temporary fix. My tormented memory had returned—much to my chagrin, but by this time I had taken on new fears. Not that the old ones were gone—I had just added new ones to the list. Fear of some dread disease taking my life or the life of one of my loved ones, fear of my husband having to go to war, fear of an accident claiming the life of a family member... these and many others plagued my every waking moment! Every ambulance siren and every late night phone call sent terror through my entire being. Each day became just a dreaded blur.

I think what I regret most were the special moments in my husband's career and in the lives of our children that I missed. During all of this emotional turmoil my husband was trying desperately to hold together the Pepsi Cola Bottling Company that his father had started before he was born. To keep up with the times, he felt that he needed to build a new production plant. When the contractor went broke in the middle of the project, I vaguely remember Jack having to take on the responsibility of finishing the task within an unbelievably tight budget.

Years later he told me of an incident during this time when he burst into tears while talking to one of the top Pepsi executives from New York who was putting excessive, unfair demands on him. (The calls were attempts at forcing small independent bottlers like him to sell.) Like most men he was humiliated, but the uncalled-for stress from the New York office—on top of the strain he was under at home—just suddenly went over the top. The man he was talking with, not knowing exactly what to say, made an excuse and got off the phone. It turned out to be a minor blessing in disguise. The tears released some of the immediate stress, and that particular Pepsi official never called to harass him again.

Somehow, with God's help Jack was able to successfully finish the building project, and the dignitaries from the Pepsi Company in New York came to Brownwood to host a giant Grand Opening. What should have been the awesome privilege of sitting by my husband on the platform and proudly watching him receive well deserved honors, turned out to be a haze in my mind as I watched from a distance, hoping not to be noticed. Without the faithful help of my mother, I would not have even remembered the importance of my dressing up for the occasion, but in an attempt to help me appear as normal as possible, she bought me a dress and a pair of shoes and never left my side throughout the entire festive occasion. I had become totally self-centered—not in a prideful way—but nonetheless, I was still hopelessly self absorbed. I could not feel his world—just my own.

After several years had passed since the shock treatments, Jack decided to take me back to Dr. Ezell for more. Even though he was paying out more money in psychiatric fees than he was making, he told the doctor, *"Just get her well. Don't draw it out. Whatever it costs, I will find a way to pay you. Just get her well."*

It was at that point that Dr. Ezell explained to Jack that he couldn't guarantee that I would ever be better. He told Jack that he could expect me to be on some kind of anti-depressant the rest of my life and that he only hoped that he could keep me stable enough not to have to be institutionalized. Of course, I was not told any of that at the time, but Jack told me later that he had never felt as hopeless in his life as he did at that moment.

Jack had questioned him at the time, *"You're the psychiatrist. Why can't you get her well?"* And Dr. Ezell had made a statement that is very significant. He said, *"There is no psychiatrist around who can treat the **cause** of the illness because medical science doesn't **know the cause**. We can only treat the symptoms."* There was more truth to that statement than what we realized at the time.

Needless to say, Jack went home that day even more devastated than I was. I thank God for a wonderful husband. Most young men would have left their wives at that point. I look back now and realize that he just saw it as his responsibility to take care of me, and that he did—for over eight long years.

Thinking that I might harm myself, the doctor had left instructions that I was to be supervised at all times. But what they didn't know is that, even though there were times when I thought I couldn't take the emotional and mental torment another moment, I never once considered suicide because of the obsessive fear that I might find myself in eternity, locked in that state of agony.

Chapter 2

THE ROAD HOME

Eight years of torment had passed, and one particular night, after thinking how long it had been with no hope of improvement, I remember becoming so miserable that I couldn't stand to stay inside the house another minute. The next thing I knew, I found myself at the clothes line, crying out, *"Lord, if there even is a God, and if You are really there, find me and bring me back to You."* I recall that I didn't feel a thing. I had just verbally given up completely, **maybe for the first time**. Nothing I had ever tried had worked, and I had literally tried everything. For eight long years I had searched for Him with my mind, and this was the first time I searched for Him with my heart.

I look back in retrospect and realize that God went immediately to work on that request at the clothesline, but at the time I was too much in despair to see it. All the time that I thought I was the one doing all the searching for God—He was, in fact, the One searching for me.

It was the very next week in 1971, that Jack had to go to New Orleans to a Direct Cost Accounting Seminar for Certified Public Accountants, and my parents kept our two children so that I could go with him. (During the few months of temporary relief right after those first shock treatments, we decided to have another baby. Neither of us had wanted our daughter to be an only child. Jack had also thought that a sibling would bring a little more normality to Angelia's life.) My parents, who were always trying to help, were confident that a change of surroundings would do me good.

The first night Jack and I went as far as Austin, Texas, and stayed with some old high school classmates. Even though we had long since quit doing much socializing with friends, we would see this couple from time to time. But this was the first visit when they had ever mentioned the experience Jesus referred to in Acts 1: 4-5. We stayed up until 2 a.m. that morning just like little hungry birds— picking their brain with every question we could think of. I remember an excitement rising up on the inside of me as I kept hoping against hope that this experience might be the answer to my problem. Even after we went to bed that night, I couldn't sleep because of the exuberance I felt.

After leaving Austin the next day, we went as far as Conroe, Texas, so that Jack could attend the

Board of Director's meeting of the Conroe Pepsi
Canning Company of which he was a director.
Since he never left me alone for any length of
time, he dropped me off at my cousin's home to
stay with his new bride, whom I had never met. I
hadn't been in the house much over five minutes
when she began to tell me exactly the same things
that the couple in Austin had told us the night
before. I was dumbfounded! I had never heard
these things before, and now—twice within
twenty-four hours—I was hearing it from two
different sources.

The rest of the way to New Orleans this *Acts
chapter two experience* was all Jack and I could
talk about. It was late in the afternoon when we
arrived, checked into our hotel and started to walk
to this little restaurant where we had good
memories from our honeymoon a little over ten
years before. On the way, however, we ran into a
Logos Book Store. We had no idea that logos
referred to the Word of God.

It was nothing short of a miracle when we went
into that bookstore and both started picking out
books to buy, because I had short-circuited and
come to the place of hating to read. I had spent
years frantically searching through encyclopedias,
but never reading for pleasure, so the thought of
reading a book would normally have thrown me

into a panic. That first night, however, I could hardly wait to get back to the room to read, and we read practically the entire night. Jack would go to his classes in the daytime, and I'd read all day while he was gone. It was the first enjoyment I had found in doing anything for such a long time that he even quit feeling that he had to keep coming back up to the room to check on me.

We each had a miracle. While the other men at the seminar were studying at night, Jack was reading Pat Boone's book *A New Song* and Hal Lindsay's *The Late, Great Planet Earth*. Jack is good with math, but he is not a CPA, yet he was the one who won the beautiful Grand Prize watch and several other awards for the highest scores while competing against a room full of CPAs.

By Thursday of that week it finally dawned on me that God had been orchestrating everything that was happening. I remember just glancing at the clock in the hotel room, and the next thing I knew I was pouring my heart out to God, *"Lord, I don't even know how to ask, but I want what our friends in Austin, and my cousin in Conroe, and these people I'm reading about have!"* And as I lay back across the bed this heavenly prayer language just began pouring out of me. The next time I looked at the clock, forty minutes—that seemed like only a moment or two—had passed. I had never experienced that kind of peace in my life. In fact, it had been so long since I had experienced any semblance of peace that I thought, *"Lord, this is so good. I never want it to end."*

For some reason I didn't tell Jack what had happened that night. It was like I was afraid to talk about it for fear of losing it. At dinner I kept leaving the table to go to the restroom, desperate to see if I could still speak in my prayer tongue. I felt giddy like a young school girl who had just laid eyes on her first love. After dinner that night I was too excited to read, so I finally just floated off to sleep while Jack read. It was on the way home the next day that he shared with me what had happened to him the night before. Just as he began to drift off to sleep, he started praying in his prayer tongue. Thinking that maybe he was dreaming, he jotted some of the words down in the margin of his book that was lying on the nightstand and went back to sleep. When he got up to go to the seminar, I noticed his flipping desperately through the pages of his book. I asked what was wrong and he assured me that everything was fine, yet I could see he was let down about something. Later that morning I picked up my book to read and found all of these strange words scribbled in the margin. In the dark, he had written in my book by mistake! That next morning when he couldn't find his scribbled notes, he thought maybe he had just dreamed it. It wasn't until we started home that we began piecing together what had happened. This broke the ice and we eagerly began sharing with each other what God had done. We were faced with a dilemma because we literally thought we were the only two people in Brownwood, Texas, who had even heard of this glorious encounter, much less experienced it!

With every intention of telling everyone we knew about our experience, our excitement was at a level ten. I realize now that God knew I was not ready for that kind of confrontation. Negative reactions to my newfound joy would have washed me away at that point, so God literally protected me from sharing it. Our pastor (by this time we had joined the Baptist church) was extremely busy and we couldn't get an appointment to see him, which was highly unusual. We also could never find an appropriate time to tell my parents. Finally, after realizing that it was God who was intervening, we went a year without telling anyone.

During that year Jack and I shared a magnificent *love walk* with the Lord. This drew us closer together and produced a healing in our marriage from those long years when he had, more or less, just taken care of me. The best way I can describe the next two years was like being in a *bubble of peace.* It was like I had never been sick. Credit was given to the New Orleans trip for the transformation that people saw, yet could hardly believe. Little did they know, however, that the change was from what had happened *during* the trip, rather than the trip itself.

My relationship with the Lord became so wonderful that I found myself still weeping constantly—but now, from tears of joy rather than tears of agony and hopelessness. However, after two years of a precious honeymoon time with my husband and with the Lord, I began realizing that some of those old fears were beginning to creep up again. In a desperate attempt to hang onto my newfound peace, I would push them down by frantically trying to busy myself and trying to ignore the panic that was mounting.

Knowledge of how to do spiritual warfare was still foreign to both of us. I remember crying out in desperation, *"Lord, I know You're real, but I feel the torment coming back. I have to have some help. I don't know what to do or where to turn."* I was desperately searching the scriptures and even though I really didn't understand it, I somehow knew that this certain verse I had found held the answer!

Whoever calls on the Name of the Lord will be delivered!
                                                    Joel 2: 32

Chapter 3

THE SICK NEED A DOCTOR!

One Sunday morning I was alone in my bedroom getting dressed, when suddenly and very quietly I had a *vision*. I didn't know it was a vision at the time—I just knew something supernatural was happening. I was aware that I was sitting in my bedroom. I didn't go into any kind of trance, but it was like I could see myself sitting in a chair—much like a dental chair—and a man dressed in white was standing beside me.

The man told me to open my mouth, and when I did I could see a black tooth. Then my whole body became transparent, and I saw black roots going down through the trunk of my body and down my arms and legs. Next the man reached in and pulled out the tooth with all the roots, leaving holes all through my body. After that he told me to watch what must happen, and he started packing something in those holes until they were completely full. (I didn't know until much later how significant that part of the vision was.)

Finally, I was told to open my mouth again and there was just a healed area where the black tooth had been. I was ecstatic. I thought the vision meant that the *deliverance* I had been asking for had taken place while I watched the removal of the tooth. What a relief to have this over with!

I wish it had been that simple and that instantaneous. But for the moment, I was so thrilled that all I could think about was finding Jack and telling him what had happened. One heavenly, blissful night, just rejoicing in the Lord, was spent before the bottom fell out spiritually the next day. I can't even remember what initiated it, but before I knew it, I was emotionally as tormented as I had ever been. It was like the last eight years came crashing back upon me in an instant.

I can remember going to the medicine cabinet and spilling medicine bottles all over the floor in a desperate attempt to, hopefully, find an old bottle of anti-depressant pills. I had not taken one of those pills for over two years, but now I was in near hysterics. I went into a panic attack, frantically trying to think of something to do to keep myself from going back into the pit out of which I had come. I forgot the vision! I forgot the two year bubble of peace that I had experienced! I forgot everything!

By this time we had met a couple, Grady and Pat Chastain, who had become our prayer partners, and I didn't realize that they, and Jack, were desperately looking for someone who could help me. I also didn't realize that God was *still* orchestrating circumstances *to find me and bring me back to Him*—in answer to the prayer I had prayed at the clothesline two years before.

After finding a pastor and his wife, Bert and Charlene Maxfield, who believed in deliverance, our prayer partners went to Jack with some cassette tapes the Maxfields had given them on demons and deliverance. I found out later that he had thrown the tapes down, resolutely saying, "*I will not be a demon chaser.*" However, when I continually got worse, he finally went searching for those tapes and said, "*I'll try anything.*"

Pastor Maxfield asked us to pray and fast for three days and nights. We had never even missed a meal before, so we couldn't imagine going three days without food, however, it must have been supernatural because neither of us ever even felt a hunger pain. I can't truthfully say that I had any faith to believe that this would work, but it was like I had no other choice. I had tried every other avenue, and by this time I was numb, just simply going through the motions.

On the evening of the third day we met with Pastor Bert and his wife and our prayer partners, Grady and Pat. I had never read a book or heard a tape on deliverance, so I had no preconceived ideas. In fact, I had absolutely no idea what to expect, but they began to command a spirit of fear to come out in Jesus' Name. From the stool in the middle of the room where I was sitting with my hands lifted up in praise, as I had been instructed to do, I felt very conspicuous and self-conscious until my hands and feet began to tingle so badly that the pain took my mind off my uneasiness. I didn't make the connection that it had something to do with what they were saying.

Finally, the pain moved up my legs and up my arms until I was unable to concentrate for trying to figure out what was happening to my body. Just as I was getting ready to tell them what I was feeling, I passed out. For the next twenty or thirty minutes I was completely unconscious, with no recollection of what I was later told had happened. (I need to say at this point that every salvation experience is unique and every deliverance is unique. Probably most deliverances are not as dramatic as mine.) I was told that I began to scream so loudly that they were afraid the neighbors would call the police or come over to see what on earth was going on. In all the eight years I had never had an emotional outburst. I had actually turned into being an introvert. Yet I remember the excruciating pain I felt in my arms and legs as they prayed for me.

To muffle the sound as much as possible they went bounding through the house trying to pull down windows and close curtains. They even ripped my drapes in the den while trying to force them closed, instead of finding the drawstrings.

When I came to, I was lying on the floor and I couldn't move. My legs were pulled up against my body and my arms were drawn up like someone with an extreme case of crippling arthritis. I remember that the pain was almost unbearable. My face was numb and my lips were drawn up in a tight little round circle as though I were trying to whistle. I remember thinking, *"I can't move any part of my body and the pain is excruciating, but I have absolutely no fear."* Jack was white as a sheet, and he said that the only thought that was going through his mind, seeing me frozen in this position, was, *"Oh, Lord, don't let my mother-in-law come. How would I ever explain this to her?"*

I was looking up at the ceiling and I had—not a vision, but a very vivid mind picture. I was in the Throne Room asking Jesus, *"Why don't You do something to help me."* And the Lord said something very significant that I have never forgotten. He said, *"I have done all I am going to do. I have already done it all on Calvary."* With those words the pain left and peace just flooded my being. In fact, this was the first time I had felt the sensation of the torment actually leaving. They continued to cast out spirits for another two hours or more, and God's anointing was obvious as they called out spirits they could not possibly have known about in the natural.

After we went to bed that night, Jack and I talked for hours. We knew that the most phenomenal thing in the world had just happened and we couldn't share it with anyone. Who would believe it! Our torn curtains, however, proved that we hadn't been dreaming. Actually, we had no idea that anything like that existed in the entire world.

We had stumbled onto something that Jesus had taught those first disciples to do. What psychiatry, well meaning people, mind over matter and even those who loved me most could not do, Jesus had done for me in one night's time.

Chapter 4

RENEWING THE MIND
The Exchange System of Thoughts

I felt numb, but very peaceful. There was no doubt that God had supernaturally delivered me. I had never experienced anything like that in my life, neither had I known anyone else who had ever experienced anything even similar. **However, about noon on the third day I started having some of the same thoughts and feelings and fears that had plagued me so many times before.** I was confused and frightened. I knew that what had happened in my deliverance was real, but why didn't it take care of the problem? Why were some of the old feelings still plaguing me? (I am taking you through the entire scenario to explain the progressive steps I went through before I found *lasting* victory. Without understanding the process many people never go on to get total freedom.)

The Lord brought back to my remembrance the part of the vision where the cavity from the extracted tooth had to be packed. He impressed me that the packing was as important as pulling the tooth (the deliverance itself). It had not taken long at all to pull out the tooth, but the emphasis of the vision had obviously been on the packing because of the length of time it had taken to push the gauze into the cavity left throughout my body from where the infected tooth had been.

Somehow God revealed to me that the *renewal of the mind* was what the packing period in the vision had represented. Demon oppression had been delivered out of my mind and emotions, but now it was necessary that those holes not be left empty. They had to be packed with *truth* from God's Word.

From that moment the Spirit of God supernaturally directed me step by step. I spent the next several months just sitting in a chair with my Bible and notebook in my lap, soaking up the Word. The Holy Spirit led me to see spiritual warfare revealed in Scripture like I had never seen it before. In fact, the things that the Lord revealed to me from His Word during those months are the very notes that the Lord had me later type up to use as a handout for people we would take through deliverance. I called that handout *Things I found helpful in keeping my*

Deliverance because that is exactly what it was—information that was so simple, yet so crucial and indispensable that I couldn't survive without it, even today.

One of the things God spoke to me was that I must make the Word of God my *final authority* in every area of my life, and I remember how impossible that sounded at the time. I reasoned that there were things in the Bible that went so contrary to the world that I couldn't imagine being able to function in this life and rely totally on the Word at the same time. It would be like trying to live in two different worlds simultaneously.

It was during this period of time that a friend invited me to go with her to hear a prophet who was ministering in this little church across town. I had never heard of a modern day prophet, therefore, I was without a clue. And to be honest, the only reason I consented to go was out of curiosity. The church was full and the only place I could find to sit was in the middle of one of the back pews, so I certainly was not in a conspicuous place.

During the ministry time the prophet pointed straight at me and asked if I would come forward because the Lord had a *Word* for me. I had never heard a prophecy before. I had no idea what to expect, but I certainly was not anticipating the gamut of emotions that followed. The Lord began to say through this prophet, "*God wants you to make up your mind that you are going to choose to believe His Word. God wants you to decide that you are going to make His Word your final authority. God just wants you to make a choice to believe Him over everything else. God wants you to make up your mind that from this day forth you are going to choose to believe His Word.*"

I don't know how many times that was repeated (maybe once for each 10,000 times I had doubted the Lord), but it sounded like a broken record, and my first wave of emotion was *embarrassment* over what all these people must be thinking. Finally, I forgot the people and started listening to what was being said. God was telling me *how to do* what I had been told to do earlier. He was giving me the *secret* for making the Word my final authority. Instantly, something inside me just clicked, and I realized that it was merely a choice—just a simple *decision* to believe God's Word, and I didn't have to *feel* anything. So standing there in that little church that night, **I determined in my heart to make God's Word my final authority—the most liberating thing I have ever done in my life.**

After I passed that first hurdle, the Word gradually started coming alive. God began to show me the schemes of the enemy over my life, and He spoke the words *"exchange system"* to me. As simple as this little exchange system sounds, it is the way in which we can win the battle against the enemy every time. No matter what the battle might be, every single time it will start in the mind and affect the emotions. It will be the same dynamics—no matter what area is being hit.

> *The thief comes to steal, kill and destroy, but I have come that you might have life and life more abundantly.* John 10: 10

I am going to explain the exchange system in a nutshell because it is so effective. **The Lord showed me to take every thought that did not line up with the Word of God—every thought that tried to steal my peace, rob my joy or destroy in any way—and exchange that negative thought for a thought from God's Word.** He impressed me that the exchange system works no matter what the thought might be—a thought of sickness, fear, despair, insecurity, jealousy, divorce, lust…whatever. I was to take the contrary thought and exchange it for a contrasting thought from God's Word. That is exactly what Paul was writing to the church at Corinth.

> *Take every thought captive to the obedience of Christ and pull down the strongholds*

and lofty things raised up against the know-
ledge of God.   2 Corinthians 10: 4-5

When I first started taking these negative
thoughts captive, it took a great deal of time. At
least ninety-nine percent of my thinking must have
been influenced by fears, doubts, insecurities... I
was not necessarily a negative person, but I had
formed habits of thinking on things that didn't line
up with the Word, and every one of those thought
patterns had to be exchanged if I wanted to be set
totally free.

I learned that to walk in the Spirit meant I
couldn't go by sight or circumstances. Regardless
of the situation, I had to choose to believe
whatever God said.

> *While we look not at the things which are*
> *seen, but at the things which are not*
> *seen; for the things which are seen are*
> *temporal (temporary, subject to change),*
> *but the things which are not seen are*
> *eternal.*   2 Corinthians 4: 18

It was a relief to find out that those demon
spirits were not indwelling my spirit man because
my spirit man was indwelled by the Spirit of God.
Those spirits of fear and doubt that had tormented
me for so long were in my soulish realm (mind,
will, emotions), and that was the part of me that

had to be renewed after my deliverance. That was what the *packing* of the hole left by the extracted tooth represented in my vision.

> Jesus said, "*If I cast out demons by the power of God, then the Kingdom of God can come upon you.*"   Matthew 12: 28

What is the Kingdom of God?

> *...the Kingdom of God is righteousness, peace and joy in the Holy Spirit.*   Romans 14: 17b

No wonder I could never have peace and joy. My mind and emotions were so filled and cluttered with harassing spirits. Paralyzing doubts had left little room for righteousness, peace and joy.

The enemy's subtle trap is to put thoughts in a person's mind, either directly in *first person* or through circumstances. For example, he puts thoughts like, *"I think I'm having a heart attack... I don't think I love my mate any longer... I don't think my husband loves me... on and on!"* The fact that the thought is in first person makes one assume it is his own thinking.

Also *the things that we see or hear* will trigger a thought, and immediately, that thought is accompanied with an emotion. We *feel* fearful or we *feel* despair or jealousy, and at that point, we have to be on our toes and in the Spirit. Otherwise, we will be washed away, simply because we are so accustomed to operating out of our mind, our reasoning and our emotions.

The one thing that belongs totally to us is our *will*, therefore, God will not violate our will. Your will is like the *switch*—it is your *instrument of exchange*. I was reminded of Jack's pickup truck with two separate gas tanks. When one tank became low he had a switch under the dashboard that would immediately transfer him over into the other tank. That is a good analogy of our will. Our will is our switch. With our will we can choose to switch over into the spirit by exchanging the negative thought with a thought from God's Word—or we can choose to continue dwelling on the negative thoughts. It's our *choice*. Our *will* is the switch that can immediately take us from the physical to the spirit—or to the soul (mind)—and back again, depending on which level we choose to operate.

The Lord showed me to exchange every thought of fear for one of His scripture promises. I was to exchange every thought of *sickness* for one of His promises of health. Every thought of *lack* was to be exchanged for His promise of provision. I use a favorite promise for *provision* that Paul wrote to the Corinthian church.

*And God is able to make all Grace abound
to you, that always having all sufficiency
in everything, you may have an abundance
for every good deed.* 2 Corinthians 9:8

Every thought of anger had to be exchanged for
an opposite thought from His Word.

*This you know, my beloved brethren. But
let everyone be quick to hear, slow to
speak and slow to anger; for the anger of
man does not achieve the righteousness
of God.* James 1: 19-20

Every thought of inferiority had to be
exchanged for a promise of *who I am* in Christ—
every thought of doubt had to be exchanged for a
faith promise—every thought of temptation
exchanged for a promise of His strength and
faithfulness...on and on! God wants us to be able
to say, as Jesus did in John 14: 30, *"The prince of
this world is coming but he has nothing in me"*—
none of his evil spirits are controlling me.

Salvation is an act—and then it is a process. In
the same way *deliverance* is an act—and then a
process. It is a one time experience. But it is also
an on-going progression as God continually cleans
us up. The more we get cleaned up—the more of
His peace and joy and righteousness can fill our
being. Like I said earlier—this process is what

made up the long *packing* part of my vision—after the badly infected black tooth (demonic oppression) had been removed.

Something wonderful began to evolve as I put this *exchange system* into operation. I began to experience a *love walk* that I didn't even know existed. When I saw the kind of love that would keep on loving me—after I had turned my back on Him, I was overwhelmed. He never left me or forsook me through all those years, and He kept drawing me by His Spirit though all those progressive steps until He could heal and deliver and restore what the enemy had stolen.

> *Then I will return to you the years that the swarming locust has eaten, the creeping locust, the stripping locust, and the gnawing locust.*　　　　　Joel 2: 25

A constant watchfulness is necessary because every time it appears that the Word isn't working, our flesh wants to throw up its hands and say, "I give up on God's way. It is just not working." At that point God wants to take us to the next level of healing and deliverance and faith. And probably the hardest level for me to achieve was the exchange system. Exchanging all those habitual thoughts felt, at times, like *pulling flesh off my bones*. It often seemed next to impossible to make those fear thoughts yield to what God's Word said—especially when the fears sounded reasonable and the emotions were going wild. Often it seemed crazy to believe God's Word more than what I was seeing. But if we keep submitting to God in obedience, we will eventually win.

> *Now to Him who is able to do exceedingly and abundantly beyond all that we ask or think according to the power that works within us.*   Ephesians 3: 20

When the exchange system—after much practice—started becoming second nature, the next blessing that came was truly exceedingly and abundantly beyond anything I could have even known to ask for. **The torment (which kept recurring even after the intervals of relief from having received the infilling of the Holy Spirit and experiencing deliverance) finally left and never returned.** I have to remind myself what it was like during those eight years. It is like remembering what some close friend from years ago went through. At last, my house was no longer left empty for the enemy to again try to occupy. This scripture in James started to make sense.

> *Submit therefore to God. Resist the devil and* **he will flee from you.**   James 4: 7

It was God's Power that accomplished the victory, but I had a part to play. He showed me that the determining factor to any person's getting completely well is his willingness to obey and not give up on God anywhere along the way. I personally found out, for a certainty, that *those who call upon the Name of the Lord will be delivered (Joel 2:32)!*

Even today, when I think of how God has used me to help people all over the United States to overcome the very problems that plagued me so unmercifully at one time, I cannot quit thanking Him for His immeasurable Grace. He has turned my life around to become just the opposite of those eight years. In fact, there are times when it is hard for me to believe that I'm that person who lived back there in torment.

Chapter 5

PART II: KEEPING DELIVERED

An Ounce of Prevention Is Worth A Pound of Cure!

*When the unclean spirit goes out of a man, it passes through waterless places seeking rest, and not finding any, it says, "I will return to my house from which I came." And when it comes, it finds it **swept and put in order.** Then it goes and takes along seven other spirits more evil than itself, and they go in and live there; and the last state of that man becomes worse than the first.* (emphasis added)
Luke 11: 24-26

...but be filled with the Spirit.　　　Ephesians 5: 18

My objective for Part Two in this book is to show other people who are held in bondage how to *get set free*, and more importantly, to teach Christians how to *stay free* by avoiding Satan's traps in the first place. However, it is not enough to direct a life to be *minus* the oppression, but to encourage one to be *filled up*. Interestingly, it is in keeping oneself filled up that prevents further oppression. So the goal is not *being swept clean, put in order and left EMPTY*. The goal is the infilling. I had a supernatural deliverance so it was obvious that my life was cleaned out and reordered. However, without the verse in Luke 11, one might never know that **a successful deliverance does not guarantee lasting freedom**. If the house is swept clean and left empty that invites trouble in the spiritual realm.

Consider this analogy: A city that has already been occupied by the enemy is very difficult to liberate. The enemy becomes intertwined with the inhabitants, and it is no insignificant matter to free that city. The longer the infiltration, the more the culture has mixed. In the same way our soulish lives have learned habits from the occupiers. The longer a person has been under the influence of a spirit, the more the soul has been tainted. The best possible scenario is to *prevent* an occupied state. It is much easier to *keep* the enemy out, rather than to *put* him out. Sin is an occupier of space. No matter how hard it is to hold the territory and keep it free of intruders (sin), ultimately, *prevention* is much easier than *recovery*.

...whatever is not from faith is sin. Romans 14: 23

I certainly do not want to discourage anyone who already has occupied territories by making it sound as though it is too late. My life is a prime example that total deliverance can come, no matter how oppressed one might already be. But it is still a fact that prevention is easier than recovery.

There are all types of prayers: prayers of resistance, prayers of relinquishment, prayers of persistence... But, from experience, my favorite type of praying is *preventive* praying. *Lord, lead me away from temptation, deliver me from evil!* This is a type of praying that is **ahead of time** praying—preventive medicine—action taken *before* the calamity strikes. How much better, before the city is taken, for one to pray that God would actually pick him up and take him out of the pathway of harm. One needs to so completely fill himself with the Word of God that a puncture wound would find only the Word flowing out.

Submit therefore to God. Resist the devil and he will flee from you.   James 4: 7

*For I know that nothing good dwells in me, that is, in my flesh; for the wishing is present in me, but the doing of the good is not. For the good that I wish, I do not do; but I practice the very evil that I do not wish. But if I am doing the very thing I do not wish, I am no longer the one doing it, but sin which dwells in me. I find then the principle **that evil is present in me**, the one who wishes to do good. For*

*I joyfully concur with the law of God in the inner
man, but I see a different law in the members of my
body, waging war against the law of my mind, and
making me a prisoner of the law of sin which is in
my members. Wretched man that I am! Who will set
me free* (**deliver me:** King James Version) *from the
body of this death? Thanks be to God through
Jesus Christ our Lord.* Romans 7: 18-25a

My son in law, who played starter lineman in a
football crazy town, had this thought race through
his mind right before one of the major playoffs his
Junior year, *"I'm going to get my knee injured."*
Within an hour of having that thought, he was
being put in an ambulance—unable to enjoy not
only the glory of playing in that important game,
but also forfeiting the pleasure of being able to
play in the state championship his senior year. It
would have been impossible to have anticipated
the sting that lay ahead of him—surgery and
excruciating pain, the financial expense, the
disappointment of being refused into the Marine
Corps, the years of constant precaution to avoid a
re-injury, and the struggle now to believe for a
healing from an "occupied" state. David will
openly tell you that he wishes he had known to
initially take the few minutes, years ago, to deal
with that subtle premonition and attack it with
scriptures. If he had done what we are going to be
talking about in the next few chapters, it would
have saved him an incalculable amount of

problems. Our initial response to warning flags is by far the easiest way to overcome.

In the same way, when everything lies broken around a person and he feels the throbbing pain of his injured hand, the tantrum could have been dealt with and avoided at the thought stage. How much better to have kept the enemy out, rather than now having to deal with him from an "occupied" state!

In Christopher Clayton's testimony (on page 182) he says this so well, "As anyone knows who struggles with drug addiction, it changes from a *"want to"* to a *"have to."* We don't see this line in front of us and choose to step over it; rather, we look behind us, and there it was. If Satan had shown me where I would end up before I took my first drink or hit, I would have said, *No!* If I could have caught a glimpse of the misery I would endure in the future, I would have said, *No!"* An ounce of prevention *truly is* worth a pound of cure.

I've read many books describing individual deliverances in which very good arguments were made, convincing the reader of the *need* for deliverance. I have not, however, found a book explaining in detail how to keep one's deliverance. After my intense struggle, I am convicted that instruction of that kind is equal in importance to the deliverance itself, therefore, in the next chapters I will be giving you what I call crucial information for obtaining and maintaining your freedom.

Hopefully, the remaining chapters in this book will present valuable steps for overcoming the enemy in such a simplistic manner that you will see the answers, as not only feasible, but simple enough to easily adopt.

Chapter 6

Don't Ignore Satan: Answer Him!

Are you aware that there is no place in the Word of God that tells us to ignore Satan? We are told to *resist* the enemy, but we are never told to *ignore* him. At the first *feeling* of something coming on or at the first oppressing *thought*, resistance with the Word needs to be the initial response. When my world felt like it was caving in on me and my only thought was to run for my medication or to give in to the temptation to dissolve in fear, the oppression would linger for weeks, and sometimes even months. However, when I felt it coming on, if I would persistently quote God's Word—those *"feelings"* would actually lift within the hour. Power over the enemy has been given to us! No matter how strong the attack may feel—demon oppression does not have power over us unless we give in to it.

The very opening stage of man in the Bible is a scene of spiritual warfare (Genesis 3:1-5). In verse two Eve is quoting God's Word. Then the enemy quotes it back, contradicting what God had said. Eve lost that initial battle, but when the second Adam came on earth, He reenacted this very event, this time carrying it out correctly. Jesus replayed the episode, doing what Adam and Eve should have done, and at the same time showing us exactly what to do when we find ourselves in spiritual warfare. In Matthew 4: 3 when the enemy came to tempt Jesus, He didn't think, *"Oh, it's just the devil. I don't have to listen to him. I have more power than he does, therefore, he doesn't matter."* Do you realize here that Jesus took the devil very seriously? Sometimes as Christians, because we know the power behind us is greater, we assume that we don't have to pay any attention to the devil. Therefore, we are prone to ignore, rather than resist.

I don't think it is any coincidence that the temptations in this reconstruction of the scene in the Garden were almost identical to the ones presented to Eve. The first temptation of Jesus was to *turn the stones into bread.* The counterpart in the Garden was *eat the fruit from the tree*—both offering satisfaction of immediate desires.

The second temptation, challenging God's integrity, was *jump from the temple and see if God is telling the truth when He says you won't die.* To Adam and Eve the temptation was—*you can eat the fruit. Don't pay any attention to God. You won't die!* Satan tries to make man think that he is invincible, and in and of ourselves we cannot defeat the devil. The victory comes from knowing that *Greater is He that is in me than he that is in the world (I John 4:4)* and putting our authority to work.

The third temptation from the devil was *–I will give you **all the earthly kingdoms** in exchange for bowing down and worshipping me.* It was an offer of *power.* Remember the corresponding offer in the Garden—*if you eat this fruit you will be like God—equal to God.*

Alone on the mountain and in a weakened condition, Jesus did what Adam and Eve should have done and showed us once and for all what we should do. **He did not ignore the enemy—He resisted with the Word.**

There is an important clue that I want you to remember. Just as the rattlesnake rattles a warning before he strikes, there is also a rattle that the enemy gives out before his attacks. If we watch for his rattle we will not be caught off guard. The rattle will often come in the form of a subtle thought. It is a fleeting, almost subconscious thought that can easily be missed if we haven't trained ourselves to watch for it. (We'll talk more about this in chapter eight.) Other times the rattle will come as an uptight "feeling" on the inside.

Let me give you some examples of the enemy's warning rattle! Have you ever been feeling good and the thought crossed your mind, *"Things are going so well—it's almost too good to be true."* Don't ignore that thought. That is a rattle from the enemy and if we are on our toes, it is telling us that it's time to do spiritual warfare. *God has plans for our good, for a future and a hope,* but we are living in a world that is still being harassed by an enemy. When that subtle thought comes, cover your blessing with prayer. The devil likes to strike when things are going well. Instead of just *thinking* how good life has been lately—begin *thanking* God for His goodness. *Praise* is a spiritual weapon. Praise the Father for every good gift and pray for a blood covering over it.

I was talking to a lady on the phone recently and she mentioned a doctor who had accomplished marvelous things for her friend who had cancer. A very subtle, fleeting thought crossed my mind, *"I need to get that doctor's name in case I ever need him."* I immediately recognized that warning rattle. When I got off the phone, I took my Psalm 91 covenant and did warfare with *the thought of getting cancer.* There would have been nothing wrong with putting the doctor's name in a file in the event that I might later be ministering to someone who had cancer and needed the information. But this time I knew that would not have been the motive for getting his name. It was a subtle *fear rattle* that needed to be *exchanged* for a thought from God's Word.

You will have little, subtle warning flags from time to time and when you see or hear one, don't ignore it—take authority over it. The crucial timing in spiritual warfare is your first reaction to that warning signal.

Over the last thirty years we have had the opportunity to work with different ones who were plagued with seizures. Two people, in particular, come to mind. In both cases the one suffering the oppression said that he had a few moments of notice before the seizure would take over. It was not an overnight victory, but in time, each was taught how to quote the Word and take authority over the attack. So often it seems easier to give in rather than stand, but that only gives the enemy a stronger foothold the next time. *Desperate, determined people are the ones who eventually get the victory—ones who want deliverance as much as a drowning person wants his next breath of air.*

I don't have to tell you that demonic spirits can upset a whole household. When any member of the house is oppressed, the entire household is affected. In Matthew 15: 22-28, it was a *desperate, determined* mother (after putting up with much harassment, I'm sure) who saw deliverance come to a distressed daughter, simply because she was willing to humble herself and take even the crumbs from under the table, if need be.

I've been on both sides of the issue—I know what it feels like to be under oppression and to be free from it. Needless to say—free is better! But victory doesn't come because we *want* freedom. Victory comes because we are desperate to the point of doing whatever it takes to get it. So don't ignore those warning signs. Answer the enemy with God's Word.

I remember some thirty years ago when the entire family was standing out in the street watching my parent's home burn. One of the neighbors came over to tell us that two weeks earlier he had seen their home burning in a dream. His conversation did nothing except frustrate me. God does not give us a dream so that we can stand there and say, "I told you so!" or "Oh, I already knew that!" If God gives you a dream of something bad happening, it is so that you can do spiritual warfare to prevent the tragedy.

I have known people who lived through a terrible accident and told me that earlier they had a premonition that it was going to happen. That premonition, as the world calls it, is a snake rattle so that you will do spiritual warfare. **Don't ignore Satan; answer him!**

The Bible is given to us to build Godly convictions in our heart so that we can in faith resist the devil. Laziness will get us killed. No one ever *feels* like doing spiritual warfare. If we are waiting until we feel like resisting the enemy, we will probably never do it. Satan will dismantle our lives if we ignore him by failing to listen and do something with those subtle warning signals. **Remember that there is not one scriptural promise made to the one who ignores.**

We were visiting with friends and all the children were playing in their back yard. Angie burst in to tell us that Bill was dismantling their swing set, but because he was only two we really didn't pay any attention, assuming that she was over-reacting. How much harm could a two year old do to a swing set? Finally, when she came in for the third time we went out to find that he had, indeed, almost disassembled the whole thing. The children were crying as they stood helplessly watching. The slide was already on the ground and other parts were piled around as Bill sat, contentedly taking out the remaining screws with his little fingers. That episode pictures two things to me. It pictures how Satan can dismantle our lives when we ignore warnings. Angelia was warning and we were ignoring. But that scenario also pictures how a young Christian with God's ability can totally dismantle the enemy's plan.

Faith is a conviction that God's Word works. For example, when we take Psalm 91 and begin to say with conviction, *"Lord, I choose to dwell in Your shelter. You are my refuge and my fortress and You are the One who delivers me from pestilence and every evil. Your faithfulness is my shield against the enemy, therefore, I will not fear. Though a thousand may fall at my side and ten thousand at my right hand, you have promised that it will not approach me."* If we continue to stand on that until we see the results, that kind of resisting will eventually dismantle the enemy's assignment.

The majority of Christians shrinks back in fear at the thought of an enemy attack. Unfortunately however, there are many of those, even in the *minority* crowd, who are assuming that they are fighting the devil, yet they are just using *positive thinking*. Positive thinking is not one of God's divinely empowered weapons and will not work against the enemy any better than shrinking back.

Positive is better than negative, but it has no delivering power in it. Very little of what most Christians do is *spiritual warfare.* Spiritually *ignoring* has no scriptural power!

Chapter 7

Flesh Attracts Vultures

FLESH IS WHAT OPENS THE WAY TO DEMONS, therefore, it is hard to distinguish whether one is contending with demons or dealing with flesh. **I have been asked the question many times, "How do you know the difference between an area of flesh and demonic activity?"**

Let me give you this illustration. Have you ever been driving on some country road and you noticed where someone had hit and killed an animal and dragged it over into the bar ditch? After a few days, what is attracted to that dead, rotten flesh? Vultures! The more rotten the flesh becomes, the more vultures are attracted. The same thing happens in the spiritual realm. Anytime we sow to the deeds of the flesh and get into sin, we are going to reap corruption. That word corruption actually means *dead, rotten flesh.* There are vultures in the spiritual realm, and those spiritual vultures are evil spirits—demons! And just as physical vultures are attracted to physical, dead flesh, the spiritual vultures (demon spirits) are attracted to dead flesh in the spiritual realm.

Demons are attracted to those thoughts and actions and attitudes that don't line up with the Word of God. There is no way to keep demons away when a person indulges in the deeds of the flesh. That is why we can't put up with thoughts of *what can it hurt, just this once?* It does harm because if we let down once, we'll do it again, and it gets easier each time. **It is really not a question of whether it is flesh or demons. If you leave flesh there long enough, it becomes a feeding ground for demons.** That's why God tells us to get rid of our sinful flesh.

*Do not be deceived, God is not mocked... For the one who sows to his own flesh **shall from the flesh reap corruption**, but the one who sows to the Spirit shall from the Spirit reap eternal life.*
Galatians 6:7-8

The things that we do in the flesh that we consider harmless are not nearly as harmless as they appear. When we start doing things independently of God and exalting our will above the Word of God, we will reap corruption. It is a spiritual law, and it works as surely as the law of gravity.

I remember several years ago, we were talking with a man who was committing adultery, and as we were explaining what God's Word said, he simply ended the conversation by saying, "I like what I am doing, and that is what I choose to do." His mind was made up. He chose to make a decision independent of what God was saying to do. That was coming out of a *fleshly will*. He liked the forbidden territory.

When the people said to Samuel, "We want a king," (1 Samuel 8: 5) what did Samuel do? He told them all the reasons why it was not good to have a king, yet they insisted, "No, we want a king." Their will was fleshly. They were intent on choosing something outside of God's will. The flesh is always in rebellion against God. A fleshly *"will"* chooses its own way—not God's way!

We would all agree that adultery and choosing an earthly king over God are flesh and outside of God's will. But if I begin to question whether or not God is going to meet my needs—that, too, is *choosing another king*. It is doubt, and doubt is sin. One may be an extreme area of flesh that will reap more serious repercussions, but both are areas of flesh. Both will reap some degree of destruction, and eventually, open a door to the enemy.

I shall never forget the surprise in store for us the night that we, along with two other couples, consented to having a very young couple from out of town brought to us for deliverance. The wife had been in an adulterous affair, but supposedly, she had repented and wanted deliverance. Only later did it become obvious that there had been no real desire to change on her part.

We had been using our authority in Jesus' Name to call out demons for some time when Jack asked her husband to place his hand on her head and command a particular demon to quit harassing her. She was sitting in a semi-horizontal position in a recliner when the young husband walked over, stood in front of the chair, bent over and laid his hand on her head. No one could have expected what happened next. It became obvious that she was not in agreement with having that area of sin dealt with. In an instant of time, from that half lying down position, she appeared to have flown out of the chair, knocking him flat on his back, and with her legs straddling his chest, she began pounding him in the face.

Her earlier, docile countenance had been nothing more than a masquerade to disguise her anger at being brought there against her inner wishes. She wanted to appear repentant, but when one's heart is not in it, the flesh will eventually take over. Those old areas of flesh have to be cut away or they will eventually manifest, destroy our lives and make a fool out of us. What a graphic illustration of what one's flesh looks like when a demon is enticing it to manifest out of control.

Let's take *unforgiveness* as an example. Maybe we think that what a person did was so unfair that we cannot come to the place of forgiving him. And perhaps it was unfair, but if we continue to sow to that flesh of unforgiveness—it will become a feeding ground where spirits of bitterness, retaliation, hurt... begin to congregate. Where the dead carcass is, the vultures will gather! Where there is any old flesh nature left unburied, the demons will be attracted. Think about that dead animal on the side of the road—if someone buried it, it would no longer attract vultures.

By the same token, when this old flesh nature that has been crucified in Christ is left buried in Christ, it will not attract demon spirits. But when we display flesh and keep sowing to it, we will find that spiritual vultures will be attracted in the spiritual realm. Demons come to try to influence and entice in order to invade our thinking. The reason they try to tempt us is because demons enter through the flesh. **The flesh is nothing more than a feeding trough for demons.**

I once heard someone say that **flesh will do anything to keep from dying.** It will pray—work—tithe—preach! It will keep all the religious traditions, but flesh will always be an enemy of God. As long as self and Christ remain in the same heart there will be war. Self effort for selfish reasons—trying to impress someone, trying to build a name for oneself, acting out of a wrong motivation—will never bring life.

There are those who figure out in their head how to look successful in the Christian world. That is *flesh,* and it can do much more harm than good. What if I had taught a class on what I was learning while searching out the different religions? My search was gaining me a great deal of worldly knowledge that could have sounded impressive, but at that time I would have confused my listeners until they were as messed up as I was. Unfortunately, that's why some people have gone into counseling and psychology—in an attempt to work out their own problems. I never found God when I searched for Him with my mind. I found Him when I searched with my heart. Intellectual searching alone will eventually turn into fleshly pride. If my doubt and subsequent search had turned into intellectual pride from all the knowledge I was gleaning, I would never have found the truth.

When Jack and I were first married we became friends with a Bible professor who was a powerful communicator. He would use fun stories to put his point across and everyone considered him to be one of the best in his field, but he didn't see Christ as the absolute Truth, so what he taught was anchored in flesh, not in the Spirit. In this professor's mind he considered Christ to be a great teacher, just like he considered himself to be; therefore, it was prideful flesh that taught the class, and no one was drawn to Jesus.

Yet on the other end of the spectrum, our *flesh* can also say, "No!" when God *"is"* calling us to teach—or to get out of bed and have a quiet time with Him—or to do something else that He is asking us to do. The flesh will either refuse the call of God—or attempt to do it in its own way. Which ever way flesh manifests, it will eventually be a drawing card to demons. Flesh that is not pruned away is like the man who was born and died and never once cut his toe nails. That's a good picture of what it must look like in the spiritual realm.

> *The mind set on the flesh is death, but the mind set on the Spirit is life and peace because the mind set on the flesh is hostile toward God, for it does not subject itself to the law of God for it is not even able to do so.* Romans 8: 6-7

Some people are not aware of what an evil spirit is. It is a demon—a spirit being without a body. Some people hear that, but they don't take it literally, however, demon spirits are as real as you and I. But because they are *spirit* beings, they are invisible in the physical realm.

I heard a denominational pastor make this comment from the pulpit, *"If our eyes could be opened into the spiritual, we would find out that there is more going on in that realm—good and evil—than there is going on in the physical."* People tend not to be aware of activity in the spiritual domain simply because they can't see it— but it's real! Your flesh and blood body is not the real you. The *real you* is a spirit being that has a mind, a will and emotions, and you live in a physical body (a physical earth suit) which allows you to function in a physical world.

The astronauts have to wear a space suit to operate in space. In the same way we couldn't operate in this physical world if we weren't in a physical body, but even without our earth suit, we would still be a real, live being. (People get confused because it is only the physical body that we can see with our physical eyes, and man tends to believe only in what he can see.)

Demons are also real spirit beings, but because they don't have a physical body and can't be seen with the physical eye, western man tends to doubt their existence. But they are quite real—capable of thinking, capable of planning, of making decisions, of reasoning—and they have emotions and desires that they want to express. Our emotions and desires are expressed through our body. Our creativity—even our lusts—are expressed through our body, but since demons don't have a body, they need one through which to express their nature and desires. Therefore, they have to find a willing vessel. For example, a spirit of doubt has to have a person through whom it can express its doubts. A spirit of lust has to have somebody through which to express the lust. A spirit of blasphemy has to have a person's mouth through which to express that blasphemy. And those spirits will use any '*body*' that is made available to them. There was a time when Jesus cast several thousand demons into a herd of swine. They seemed to have preferred living in a pig's body to being without one at all. (Matthew 8: 31)

Once a person accepts Jesus as savior, his *spirit man* is completely and totally possessed by God. No demon spirit can invade his born again spirit, but that person can be influenced by demons in his mind, in his will, in his emotions and in his physical body. (According to Luke 13:16, a daughter of Abraham for eighteen years had a physical deformity that was caused by a spirit.) That is why we have to find ways to close the door to flesh, because areas of flesh become a feeding ground to demons. Flesh opens the door to demons. Our flesh—our self will—was crucified in Christ, but if we haven't kept the old flesh buried, it is like a decayed, rotting carcass and it attracts demons.

Christ did not come to improve our flesh; He came to replace it. Flesh cannot be disciplined and used, no more than the fat on your body can be exercised and worked on until it becomes muscle. Fat will always be fat. If we want our bodies to be in good shape, we have to get rid of the fat—not improve it. Whenever we think we can discipline our flesh, we are in will power and self control, and God says to *cut it off!* Realize that you have already been crucified in Christ. When something has been crucified, it is dead.

> *...a curse without cause does not alight.*
> Proverbs 26:2

This clearly tells us that a curse or a demon spirit cannot alight without a cause. Its only entry is through the flesh. When that dawns on us, we will start shutting some doors.

Surprise is hardly the word to describe the emotions we felt, when late one afternoon we answered a frantic knock at our door to find a man holding his wife at gunpoint and asking to be allowed into the house. Our children, who were in their early teens at the time, witnessed a valuable lesson that night, even though at the time, I wished they were anywhere, but there. We found out later that an *all points bulletin* had been put out for his arrest for the abduction of his wife with a deadly weapon. Reflecting back on the situation, I had never seen two people together with such opposite expressions on their faces: His—sheer torment and pain; hers—stark terror.

This young man was an available body for demon spirits to use for several reasons: (1) He was not walking with the Lord. In his younger years he had made a profession of faith, therefore, he was not possessed, but when one has neglected his spiritual commitment to the Lord, he has automatically made himself more vulnerable and available to demon spirits. (2) There was a curse handed down in his blood line that had never been broken.   (3) He was in total lack of knowledge concerning demons and spiritual warfare. (4) During a crisis he had fallen into the habit of yielding to his emotions, without even considering what God would have him do.

All of the above had culminated in the events that led up to his impulsive decision. During a fit of anger he brought his wife at gunpoint to have us take her through deliverance.   Jack, who is much calmer than I during a crisis, simply invited them into the den and began defusing the crisis by asking questions. It is amazing how calming the effect can be when someone is given the opportunity to get his frustrations out in the open. Gradually, the young man relaxed and, in time, had become comfortable enough to put his gun down, much to the relief of everyone in the room.

It was a very surprised young man who found that it was he, rather than his wife, who needed a great deal of deliverance.

I never cease to be amazed at the difference in countenance that takes place after a true deliverance session. We had an entirely different young man sitting in our den than the one who had come through the door several hours earlier. He was even willing for Jack to take him and his wife to the sheriff's office where, thankfully, all the charges were dropped. Without the delivering power of the Lord, that happy story would have had an entirely different ending. All of us have areas of flesh that have to be taken care of, or we will find that, in time, it is an open door to demonic oppression.

I once heard this illustration: a mouse has something inside of him that likes cheese. Someone has to recognize that desire inside of that mouse and place that cheese in just the right spot to attract that mouse. There is an old *Adamic nature* inside of us that has been crucified when we belong to Christ, but the memory of that nature is there. The enemy tries to put that cheese (temptation) in just the right place to entice and lure us. That is what evil spirits do. They know us. Paul says very plainly in Ephesians 6: 12 that our fight is against wicked spirits, and he tells us not to be ignorant of their schemes (2 Corinthians

2: 11). They know us and understand our potential weaknesses, and they plan strategies against us because they are real beings.

The number one aim of Satan's plan is to keep you from Christ. If he misses that target, then his second aim is to keep you from serving Christ effectively. The things in your life that entice and distract you are not coincidental. How many of you have ever become interested in a TV program or in a movie and you were wide-eyed until 2 o'clock in the morning? But several nights later when you decided to read your Bible and get in some study time, before nine o'clock you couldn't keep your eyes open! We've all *been there, done that!* These things are not accidental. Satan has schemes!

You may be thinking, *"What can it hurt to occasionally use my plan B or to reason something out apart from God's Word? What can it hurt if I blow off a little steam every once in awhile? After all, I'm entitled—I'm doing it right most of the time! What can it hurt to indulge in a little self pity every so often? What can it possibly hurt to spend this week in the TV and take a little break from my Bible study routine? I don't plan to make a habit of it."* That is like the person who takes his first drink or smokes just one cigarette. It establishes something in the spiritual realm. Any time we sow to the flesh, we will reap some degree of corruption.

Walk in the Spirit and you will not fulfill the desires of the flesh. Galatians 5: 16

Notice that it does not say that if you will not fulfill the desires of the flesh, then you can walk in the Spirit. You walk in the Spirit in order to be able to resist the desires of the flesh.

A well-known evangelist made this statement about demons: *"They (demon spirits) are intelligent beings who plot and plan, work out how to frustrate you, how to defeat you, how to keep you miserable, how to make you sick, and, if possible, to kill you."*

Jesus very simply said exactly the same thing in John 10: 10—*the thief (that includes all his demon powers) comes to steal, to kill, and to destroy.* Most people take that statement too lightly. What Jesus was saying is very literal. But in the counterpart to that—Jesus said, *"But I have come that you might have abundant life."* And the way we have that life is by thinking and acting dependently upon God rather than independently on our own.

Until we recognize demon spirits to be real enemy beings, waiting to take advantage of our flesh (not imaginary figments of someone's imagination), we will go right along with their game plan because of our lack of knowledge. Their targets are those unrenewed areas in our lives that we've pushed aside and not dealt with. **And that is easy to do because it is more pleasant to think about those areas where we have obtained victory.** But when we realize that particular, unconquered area is the strategic place that the enemy has targeted against us personally to destroy us, we will much more quickly do something about it. Suddenly, we won't be saying, "Oh, well, what can it hurt this once?" No! We will be saying, "That's an area that Satan has targeted in my life to destroy me, and it is as deadly as a rattlesnake, and I am determined to do something about it."

The first step is in realizing that the enemy is real and that he can and will do us damage until Galatians 2: 20 becomes a reality in our spirit man.

I have been crucified with Christ; and it is no longer I who live, but Christ lives in me; and the life which I now live in the flesh I live by faith in the Son of God, who loved me, and delivered Himself up for me. Galatians 2: 20

That is the only road to victory because until we realize that our old flesh nature has been crucified –it's dead—we will keep opening the same doors of flesh and selfishness, and demons will continue to come and feed on those old fleshly areas. And it is all because we are not fully aware that deliverance has already been provided.

Demon vultures will not bother you all that much when there is no dead flesh on which to feed. But when one sees a fleshly mind that is already doubting God's Word and rebelling against God's will to some degree, skeptically standing back and questioning God's way, it is an attraction with a flashing neon sign to the enemy. It is a demon feeder. And those demons are there to add more fuel to the fire—to add more doubt. They must have a body to operate through because if they can keep those doubts fueled, they know they can eventually control that individual's thinking and maneuver him in the direction they want him to go.

Demon spirits are in the atmosphere, circling constantly, just like real vultures, and when they begin to see and smell that old dead flesh being resurrected, they are smart enough to see the possibility of an open door. Immediately, they are attracted and they come to take advantage of the situation. On the other hand, a mind that is stubbornly and steadfastly stayed on the Word— where neither sight nor circumstances can change his mind—where the Word is going to be his final authority no matter what the situation looks like— that is no attraction to a demon.

I found seven things in the Bible that God used to illustrate the enemy. I will comment on two of them. God compared demons to flies. Matthew 12: 24 talks about Beelezbub (dung god), the lord of flies. Think about the characteristics of a fly and you can easily see why God compared them to demon spirits. A fly is very annoying. Nothing is much more aggravating than having a fly continuously buzzing around your face and in your hair. They are very distracting, and they can even pollute your food. You can have fresh food on your counter and you may have a few flies buzzing around, but if you have some stinking, rotten, decomposing food, literally hundreds of flies are attracted.

Apply this to the spiritual realm. Anytime you are thinking God's thoughts and trying to do God's will, there will still be a few demon spirits buzzing around like flies, trying to annoy you and divert your attention. Spiritually, if there is a lot of dead, rotten, decayed flesh that you are indulging in, literally hundreds of demon *'flies'* are going to be attracted, because they see an open door.

> *...some seed fell beside the road, and the birds came and devoured them... When any one hears the Word of the Kingdom, and does not understand it, the evil one comes and snatches away what has been sown in the heart.*   *Matthew 13: 4, 19*

Demons are also compared to birds that devour the seed of God's Word. Anytime there is a lack of understanding the spiritual fowls of the air come to snatch it away. Hosea 4: 6 tells us that when God's people don't know His Word, they are destroyed. Demon spirits thrive on people who operate in a lack of knowledge. When someone is not grounded in the faith, you can be assured that demon spirits are lurking nearby to see that what little spiritual knowledge they do get is stolen away. I have often observed people who hear the Word and get excited about some new truth they've learned only to be bombarded by doubts or contradictory opinions of others before the day is over. That is no accident. Those were demon spirits sent to steal the seed, just as Jesus was teaching in Matthew 13.

Years ago a young woman was coming to my weekly Bible studies, and she would get so excited every time she heard the Word. As I spoke she would follow along in her Bible, taking pages of notes, and you would hear her say under her breath, *"Oh, that's good!"* She was excited. Her spirit was bearing witness, but before she became grounded in the Word, she started dating this guy who confessed to be a Christian but was obviously not walking the walk. He knew enough of the Word to sound impressive, but he would contradict everything she was learning. Each time she excitedly shared a truth with him, he would tear it apart, and because she wasn't grounded in the Word, the fowls of the air, through that young man, stole the good Word she had received, and she fell away. Soon neither of them was going to church and eventually they began living in sexual sin.

There is such a good visual application of vultures in the Old Testament. In Genesis 15: 9-10 Abraham brought the animals that God was going to use to establish His covenant, but before the covenant was made, birds of prey came down to devour the sacrifice.

And the birds of prey came down upon the carcasses, and Abram drove them away. Gen 15: 11

What is physical in the Old Testament has a spiritual application under the New Covenant. Abram had to drive the birds of prey away to keep them from stealing his sacrifice. Look up the verse. God didn't drive the vultures away; Abraham did. There will be many times that we have to drive away the birds of prey. It is often necessary to say, *"No, you don't! In the Name of Jesus, you'll not touch the truth of God's Word to steal it from my heart. And you'll not steal the Word from my family. It is going to grow and yield a 100 fold crop* (Matthew 13:23). *"* But if we don't take that responsibility, it will be stolen.

Have you ever been antagonized by another person? Evil spirits are well capable of playing two people against each other. Jack and I learned this in a very unusual way when we first married. I was dealing with all the fears that I described earlier, and I especially battled fear when he wasn't home at the expected time. The pattern that followed was attempting at first to reason in my head why he was late—in an effort to reassure myself that everything was fine. That would work for a while, but as the hour got later, especially in the winter when it was dark early, fear would begin to really mount. Then when he finally came home, I would bombard him with, "Where have you been? Why were you so late?"

I didn't realize that all of those fear questions were coming across to Jack as just anger and control. So the enemy was punching him from the other end. When he forgot to call, he would get angry because he knew I was going to be upset. It is an unusual phenomenon that the enemy will sometimes overplay his hand, and we can find out his schemes if we're open to the Lord.

One night Jack was late. Everything had come up, and he wasn't where he could get to a phone. He later told me that on the drive home these thoughts began to rush through his mind, *"I'm late. Peggy Joyce is going to be upset."* He said that the more he thought about it, the angrier he became. The enemy was supplying him with plenty of imaginations so he had already played out the whole scenario in his head—what I was going to say and how he was going to respond. He said that the enemy had him *bouncing off the wall* by the time he actually drove into the driveway. That particular night, however, I had been unusually busy and hadn't realized how late it was. In fact, I was totally oblivious to the fact that it had been dark outside for some time, so when he came bursting through the door, I said, "Hi, honey, glad you're home. How was your day?" He was stunned. I looked up to see him with his mouth open, just staring at me with this shocked look on his face. He had his whole speech prepared.

Suddenly, it dawned on him how carefully the enemy had orchestrated the entire thing, getting him hyped up when it was all a fantasy. And, on the other end, the enemy had usually filled me with fantasy fears until I was ready to fall apart, but once we saw the scheme we never fell for it again. We started taking authority over the enemy, and interestingly, it broke the assignment. After that, Jack rarely forgot to call when he was late, but even when he did forget, I resisted the fear thoughts.

Once you see the battle plan of the enemy, be quick to join forces with your mate, or with someone else, and take authority. You'll be surprised how quickly you begin to get the victory. Demon spirits are real, and they are capable of perpetuating a successful game plan until we quit falling for it. Vain imaginations will open the door for the flesh to flaunt and display itself.

Years ago there was a comedian named Flip Wilson who became famous with his little statement—*the devil made me do it!* That, however, is not very original. As far back as the garden Eve was saying that it was the serpent that beguiled her, when, in reality, the devil can't *make* us do anything. We give him far too much credit most of the time, because he has no power compared to the power that has been given to us in Jesus' Name. He can entice and try to influence, but it is by an act of our own will when we decide to give in. We were not forced, and he cannot over-ride our free will. But if we come to a place where we've listened to him long enough to finally say *yes* to him, we have relinquished some of our authority over to him, just as surely as Adam and Eve did in the Garden.

I have had people ask, **"How can you know when you've relinquished some of your authority over to the enemy, to the point that you are fighting a demon rather than just flesh?"** I am going to give you a fairly good rule of thumb. When you come to a place where it is a compulsive drive—where you are spending a major part of your time dealing with the pressure and you absolutely cannot seem to get control—it is possibly a demon spirit. At that point it is a good guess that you most likely need some help in the area of deliverance to get the victory. Flesh will respond to your determined will and to prayer.

When the oppression is coming from a demon, authority in the Name of Jesus is the answer. And then, to keep your deliverance, you have to go back to dealing with the flesh again. You can't really separate the two because every form of flesh has a corresponding demon. By that, I am saying that you can have emotions of fear, and if you put up with that fleshly emotion long enough, there are demons of fear that are attracted to it, as surely as flies are attracted to garbage. Both the flesh and demon spirits have to be dealt with.

Jesus was able to say in John 14:30, *"The god of this world is coming and he has nothing in Me."* If demon spirits have no flesh in us to grab hold of, we, too, can say the same thing. Demons are lazy. They prefer an easy target. The more often you close the door to areas of flesh, and the more you say *"no"* to temptations, the fewer problems you are going to have with spirit harassment. Close the door to the flesh, and you have automatically closed the door to demons.

Chapter 8

Mind Vultures

The context of this book is centered around one thought that was put into my mind by a subtle, Buddhist lady—*what if the God I believe in is not the right one?* I sank to the bottom of the lake with that one thought. And I didn't resurface until eight years later.

No matter what the attack might be—whether it be against our physical body, our emotions, our judgment, our marriage, our finances, whatever—we will find that the target toward which Satan aims *first* is going to be our mind. He aims at our thought process. You have probably heard it said a thousand times that Satan's battleground is in the mind—and it is, but do you realize what his mightiest warfare *weapon* is?

Though we walk in the flesh, we do not war according to the flesh, for the weapons of our warfare are not of the flesh, but divinely powerful for the destruction of fortresses. We are destroying speculations and every *lofty thing raised up against the knowledge of God, and we are taking **every thought** captive to the obedience of Christ.*   *2 Corinthians 10: 3-5*

In this scripture you can see that thoughts are at the bottom of every attack. We are aware of where the battlefield is located, but for the most part, we are unaware of his chief weapon. Many of you are mentally going down the list of his weapons right now: sin, temptation, sickness, lack, strife, jealousy, divorce, hurt, pride... These are not, however, his primary weapons. Everything I just named is a *secondary* attack. They come as a *result* of his primary weapon. So what is Satan's key weapon? **Satan's mightiest warfare weapon is a *thought*:** *a subtle mental suggestion, an intellectual impression, a compulsive impulse, a memory recall...*

Taking into account that Satan's battleground is the mind will help us to remember that his weapon is a thought that penetrates the mind. All of the other evil things occur as a by-product of those mind thoughts—whether they are conscious thoughts or subconscious thoughts.

Failure to realize that demon spirits often come to us in the form of a thought keeps us opening the door to enemy suggestions without even realizing it. For example, a demon of fear! The thought (or the demon) comes in **first person** so we automatically assume it is our own thinking—first person thoughts like—*I must be getting the flu...* *I feel so depressed... I no longer feel like I'm in love with my mate...* And because these thoughts are in first person, we think they originated in our own mind. Nevertheless, it helps to know that Satan doesn't have many tactics other than this. He doesn't need a lot of different strategies. If he can get us to accept that thought as our own thinking, then his job is basically over—because once we receive the thought, we do the harm to ourselves.

What are the *lofty things raised up against the knowledge of God* that 2 Corinthians: 10:5 is talking about? Every idea or thought that contradicts the Word of God becomes *lofty* when we decide to give it precedence over what God says. Whatever we elevate above God becomes *raised up against the knowledge of God.*

We will also find that the battle is lost before we start if we try to handle it any way other than how verse five tells us to handle it—*taking the thought captive to the obedience of Christ.* None of our natural precautions—like keeping our mind busy on other matters, thinking positively, ignoring the thought—will ultimately work. The thought has to be taken captive *by believing what God says more than we believe the opposing thought.*

Another important fact to remember is that the enemy will always accompany these thoughts with a *feeling*. In fact, it is often the feeling that we notice first. That's no happenchance. This is the plan of the enemy to keep us from realizing there was a thought back there that started the attack in the first place, because as long as the thought is allowed to stay, it continues to do damage.

Have you ever crawled out of bed feeling down and depressed—almost engulfed in heaviness? Most of the time we are not even aware that there was a subtle thought that triggered that feeling of gloom. That is why most people just battle their *feelings*, never getting to the root of the problem, and that is exactly what the enemy wants. Whatever the emotion might be, trace it back and you will find that there was always some *thought* that triggered the sentiment.

Continuing to use heaviness as an example—it could have been any one of a hundred different thoughts that triggered it—*I'm not getting any younger... Every year I am just getting deeper in debt... I feel like a failure as a parent... The more I try to do it right, the more mistakes I make... This recurring pain could be something really serious... I'm so lonely...* I haven't even scratched the surface, but the important thing to remember is that the depression is just the *product* of the thought. It is not the feeling you take captive—it is the thought that has to be identified and taken down. But the good news is—when we are obedient to do that, the feelings will eventually line up.

It is easier to understand this enemy strategy by thinking through different scenarios. For example, many people are plagued with thoughts of jealousy. Interestingly, the moment that person accepted that thought of jealousy and started to mull over it, Satan's job was basically over. That's because once the idea is accepted, the victim will take over and begin to look for any little thread of evidence he can find to prove his suspicion to be true. I'm sure you've seen this happen. A jealous thought will come, and finally, the person becomes almost obsessed. After that, everything that happens becomes a suspicion in his mind. That is what the Bible calls *vain imaginations* and *speculations*. The jealous person will meditate on all these things until he is totally preoccupied and miserable.

Next, the jealous person will begin to accuse the other person of wrongdoing. I've even seen the time when the accused party wasn't guilty, but if the blame continued long enough, he was driven to carry out the accusations that were made against him. Children do that all the time. Once a thought from the enemy is received, it works like a magnet to draw it into being until the thought actually becomes a reality.

We worked with one couple from Arkansas whose story is a textbook case. Both the husband and wife worked out of the home, but since her job was in a small nearby town, she started carpooling with several other people in the community. As time went on, the number of people in the carpool dwindled until there were times when it was only she and one other young man making the relatively short trip to work. *Horrified* is putting mildly the emotion that burst forth when she was accused of unfaithfulness with her transportation partner. I am in no way suggesting that it is a good idea for people of the opposite sex to travel together, but in this case there was no evidence whatsoever to support the accusations. It literally took months to trace the unjustified claim back to a day when the husband had a fleeting thought cross his mind that, perhaps, during this daily time spent together to and from work, a relationship might have developed. Several deliverances later, along with this teaching on Satan's mighty warfare weapon (in this case—a fearful, suspicious thought), the man was set free, but enough damage had been done to the marriage that only God's inner healing could restore harmony.

Bitterness is another prime example of how the enemy uses this powerfully evil weapon. You have seen a person who has dwelled and meditated for years on something that was done against him, or against someone he loved, and he refused to lay it down. If you notice, it is continually brought up in conversation because Satan's suggestive thoughts are obsessive. Unfortunately, the person will often continue that destructive course until a relationship is ruined or until his own body becomes so weakened that he succumbs to disease. Recent secular medical studies have linked disease to unforgiveness and bitterness. Disease can come from the negative, unconstructive thoughts in one's mind. It is so easy to see the scheme of the enemy in all of this.

When Satan puts the thought in someone's mind that there is something wrong with his health, there will be physical sensations that accompany that thinking, but it is the thought that preceded the feeling that has to be fought down.

I remember an incident that happened to me several years ago when my grandmother was in the hospital with an inflamed pancreas. That condition, of course, is not contagious, but as she began to describe the pain that she was experiencing, a very subtle fear thought—so slight that I didn't even consciously recognize it at the moment—went through my mind that I was going to encounter the same problem. If it had been a conscious thought, I probably would have recognized and handled it. But it was a very subtle, subconscious thought and I began feeling the same pain that my grandmother had described. Having no idea at the time that I was in spiritual warfare and failing to recall the ever-so-slight thought that had come when I was in her hospital room, I automatically assumed that the *pain* was the culprit. So I simply prayed about it and took authority over the discomfort, not realizing that I was only dealing with the twig.

For the next several weeks I spent a great deal of time crying out to God, *"Lord, what is wrong with my body?"* I knew the pain in the area of my pancreas wasn't just a figment of my imagination because it would often wake me up in the middle of the night. Then one day I suddenly remembered the subtle thought I'd had in the hospital, informing me that I would have the same pancreatic attack that my grandmother was experiencing. All it took was becoming aware of the thought, because when I started pulling down that lofty notion and taking it captive with the Word, almost instantly the pain left and never returned.

That little experience left me far wiser concerning the power that thoughts carry. The moment I accepted that implanted thought, it literally started carrying out its purpose.

It is imperative that those contradictory thoughts be pulled down because once they are adopted as our original thinking, then it is our own body that will work to turn that thought into a reality. The body was made to carry out what the mind dictates—unfortunately, the bad as well as the good. The body does not have the ability to discern the good from the bad. The mind does that. The body just follows the leading of the mind. Satan sends the evil thought, but once the mind accepts it, our whole being begins to respond to it. A *thought of sin* will eventually breed sin. A *thought of rejection* will ultimately bring rejection into our life. It is the same thing with a thought of failure, depression, despair, hurt, sickness, divorce... If those negative thoughts are not taken captive, they will sooner or later become constant bedfellows, producing fantasy thoughts that fan the fire. And it all starts right between our ears. I have even witnessed on several occasions where an entire church split started with one divisive thought that was never taken captive.

Ancestral curses handed down through the bloodline will often promote subtle *thoughts of dread.* For example, a case of heart disease or cancer or diabetes can be mentioned, and without being consciously aware, a person will start entertaining the subtle thought of dread, *"Oh, that also runs in my family."* I have had people actually voice the words, *"I can't seem to help my anger—it just runs in my family."* So often those subtle thoughts are the doorknobs that open the door to the curse.

I can vividly remember one particular night while Bill was still living at home when he called down to me from his upstairs bedroom. Straining to hear what he was saying, I found myself asking him to repeat several times. It wasn't until I went to bed that night that I remembered a very subtle thought of dread that had passed through my mind—*"What is wrong with my hearing? I could scarcely make out what Bill was saying. Oh, no! I remember that my dad's mother grew to be very hard of hearing as she advanced in years."* As harmless as that sounds, a thought like that can eventually open the door to a curse just waiting for an opportunity to make entry. When I saw the assignment, I jumped right in the middle of it with the Word of God and that put an end to it, but do you see how subtly the suggestion can come? Our weapon is sharper than Satan's weapon, (Hebrews 4:12) but it does us no good if we don't use it.

We have to be *on our toes* not to take in Satan's subtle, negative thought or we will buy whatever he's peddling. How often I've seen a thought of rejection cause an individual to see himself as a rejected person! That thought can actually drive the individual to believe that people are talking against him, when there is nothing farther from the truth. But nevertheless, if a person believes the lie, it will do damage. I have seen people who believed they were being rejected react in such a way that *they* appeared to be the one doing the rejecting. And it all started with a thought.

A thought of *fear of failure* has often driven an individual to do the very thing that caused him to fail. You have probably seen this in the business world. Fear of failure will frequently cause a businessman to make some unwise decision that opens the door to failure. We see this scenario in children all the time. It is quite common for a student, faced with a test, to become so dominated by *fear of failure* thoughts that he can't even concentrate to study for the test.

How many times has a need, which appeared not to be met, finally brought on the thought, "*God doesn't care about me? The Word works in other peoples' lives, but not in mine.*" If that thought takes root, it will eventually come out of that person's mouth, and when it is believed and confessed, a spiritual law (Romans 10: 9-10) is in operation, forming a barrier through which God's blessings cannot flow. How often are we creating our own prison with the thoughts that we adopt from the enemy? And many times there is absolutely no truth, whatsoever, to the thought.

I was plagued for several years with nightmares that would cause me to frantically grab Jack, yanking him abruptly out of a sound sleep. It was very frustrating that I could never remember the dream after I came awake. Jack had his own struggles from having to adjust to a rotating shift, so the constant disturbances were becoming a real detriment to him. One morning, after an unusually rough night from having put up with my nightmares, Jack came to the breakfast table at four a.m., visibly agitated. The *thought* that had finally come to him was that the nightmares must be coming from a *hidden animosity* that I felt in my heart toward him. I knew that wasn't true, but as long as he believed that thought, I knew it was going to do damage to our relationship.

When he left for work, in spite of the fact that it was still pitch dark outside, I remember running out into the pasture and falling face down in the dirt as I cried out to God for deliverance from those nightmares. I had asked many times before, but this was probably the first time that I was desperate—*frantic* might better describe my state of mind. Suddenly, a peaceful calm came over me, and I knew God had taken charge.

Later that day I started remembering the context of the dreams—episodes in which I was always pulling Jack away from some danger—pushing him out of the path of an oncoming car, jerking him away from a snake that was coiled to strike, diving on him to kill a black widow spider that crawled into his shirt... I had no sooner voiced the words, *"Why, Lord, am I having these dreams?"* when God just spoke the word, *"Over-protection!"* I was prayed for, and I have never had one of those horrible nightmares again. Nevertheless, if Jack had not found it necessary to get those thoughts of *hidden animosity* out of his mind, the ending of that story might still not have been so good.

I firmly believe there are a great many unhappy marriages, and even unnecessary divorces, which could have been avoided if the parties involved had realized that the problem started from some subtle thought that the enemy slipped into the mind that was eventually adopted as truth.

It is next to impossible to break through the barrier of a *locked-in thought*, even if the thinking is not true, until the person himself decides to deal with the thought. I have worked with different couples who were having marital problems, and if one of those partners had adopted the thought that *"ending the marriage"* was the only solution, then that particular marriage was over—unless he somehow overrode the thought of divorce.   There is nothing that anyone can say or do unless that individual cooperates and allows his thinking to change.   All of the sound reasoning, all the warnings and all the pleading on the part of the other spouse are going to be in vain unless the individual himself does whatever it takes to remove that locked-in thought and takes it captive by replacing it with what the Word of God says.

Locked-in thoughts are fortified barriers. You have probably said this, and I have too—*"Save your breath, he (she) has already made up his (her) mind."* We say that, and we know it is a fact, but have you ever stopped to actually analyze what you are saying?   You are saying that a thought, once it has been adopted, has the power within it to destroy twenty-five years of marriage, and it can! You are saying that a thought has the power within it to disease a healthy body, and it can!   A thought has the power within it to destroy one's faith in the God of the universe.   A thought has the power within it to wipe out the strongest of friendships. You have seen this happen over and over!   That is the kind of power that an evil thought carries, once it has been accepted.

I am going to make a bold statement, but I believe that it is impossible for a person who has a serious illness to ever get well—even with medical science working for him—if he continues to think on the thought, *"I'm not going to make it! I'm not going to get well! I'm going to die!"*

One friend, who loved her career and had always felt a sense of great accomplishment, talked to us about an unexpected bout with depression that had left her lifeless and miserable. Trying to get to the bottom of the problem, we questioned her thoroughly to find the *thought* that had prompted this despair. She was adamant that she had not thought on anything that could have brought on this kind of trouble. I was almost ready to give up when she suddenly remembered the incident that had, indeed, provoked the thought.

A billboard that she passed every day on her way home from work had been changed to one of a man and woman, affectionately sitting on a couch in front of a fireplace. This friend remembered a very subtle thought that had crossed her mind as she unlocked the door to her apartment that day— *"I will probably never have any one with whom to enjoy spending time in front of a nice cozy fire."* The thought had lasted for only a brief moment, but subconsciously, it had taken root and manifested in depression. That involuntary thought of sadness had to be renounced and called out before the despair could leave.

The Bible says in Proverbs 6:2—"*We are snared by the words of our mouth.*" Proverbs 18: 21 says—"*Death and life are in the power of the tongue.*" Those, of course, are true statements, but we need to remember that every *word* is preceded by a *thought*. Therefore, if we can control our thoughts, we have automatically controlled our tongue. No wonder the mind is Satan's battleground. He doesn't need any more territory than that. If he wins in that arena, he has it made. If you will remember, Satan threw the entire human race into utter chaos because of one thought that was received.

From the fruit of the trees of the garden we may eat; but from the fruit of the tree which is in the middle of the garden, God has said, "You shall not eat from it or touch it, least you die." And the serpent said to the woman, "You surely shall not die! For God knows that in the day you eat from it your eyes will be opened, and you will be like God, knowing good and evil." Genesis 3: 2-5

There is so much in this one little exchange between Eve and Satan. We realize that Satan came and tempted Eve, but so often we fail to realize that he pulled the whole thing off with just one little suggestion, once it was received.

It appeared that Eve was perfectly happy with the arrangement she and Adam had with God. She wasn't complaining. She was simply saying, "Hey, we can eat from all the trees of the garden, except one." Then Satan presented one little thought in verses four and five. *"You surely shall not die. God just doesn't want you to be as smart as He is!"* It was just one mere suggestion, but when Eve entertained the thought and received it, she started to doubt God's Word and His motives—and Satan became *the god of this world.* Once a wrong thought is received and acted upon, sin is conceived (James 1: 15). That's all it took for their authority to be transferred over to the enemy.

Jesus was betrayed by Judas because of one simple thought. In John 13:2 we see that *the devil had already put a **thought** in Judas' mind to betray Jesus.* Ananias and Sapphira lied to the Holy Spirit because of an idea placed in their minds by the enemy, and they bought into it. Peter said, "Ananias, why have you allowed Satan to fill your mind to lie to the Holy Spirit?" (Acts 5: 3) It was an adopted thought that caused them to lie.

It is so important for us to see the power a thought carries. **Negative thoughts are spiritual *mind vultures*!** That's why we need to be so careful with our thought life. Most people do not consider sinful thoughts to be wrong, as long as they stay in the mind. We would all like for our character and our spiritual maturity to be based on how we "*act*" in church on Sunday morning. That would make it easy, since we could probably all hold ourselves in check for a couple of hours while we sit in the pew and listen to a sermon, but that is not the place from which the challenge comes.

Give yourself a test. When you are all alone with your thoughts—maybe just lying in bed at night—what do you think about? When there is no one around that you have to impress, where do your thoughts naturally run? Are your thoughts self-gratifying? Are they vengeful, bitter thoughts that dream of retaliation? Are they thoughts of past hurts—reliving painful situations over and over? Maybe you have thoughts of guilt, regretting what might have been. Are your secret thoughts money hungry, greedy thoughts? Are they sad, melancholy, grief-filled thoughts? I've known people who play sad music while they relive painful memories.

Some people have violent thoughts toward themselves or toward others. Others have lustful, sexual thoughts involving someone other than their mate. Sometimes there are thoughts of unfaithfulness—thoughts of what it would be like being married to someone else. Many marriage partners mull over thoughts of no longer being turned on emotionally or sexually by the mate or thoughts of no longer being in love with the mate.

Some marriage partners are very careful not to ever verbalize it, but they entertain thoughts of divorce when they get hurt. Because those thoughts are often quite subtle, they really don't understand the trap that the enemy has been laying for them. They falsely surmise that it doesn't hurt to think about it. It does hurt. It is a trap of the enemy. Those kinds of thoughts will never allow that marriage to become God's highest. There will always be a barrier.

These *secret* thoughts are what determine the outcome of one's entire life. That kind of subtle thinking—even though it might not be in that person's conscious mind—will manifest some way in his actions. Subtle irritations toward the mate for no apparent reason often begin to crop up— sometimes sharpness in the tone of voice or a coldness in the mannerism. And if you brought it to his attention, he probably couldn't even tell you why he was irritated. But it is coming from those subtle subconscious thoughts.

We transfer our authority over our marriage, over our social acceptance, over our finances, over our physical body... to the enemy just as surely as

Eve did when we accept Satan's thoughts in any of these different areas. It is sobering when we think how easy it is to yield over our authority. Eve did it in the twinkling of an eye.

As a man thinks within himself so he is.
Proverbs 23: 7

The secret thoughts that we live with when no one else is around are literally who we are. That's our character. Our private thought life is the level of maturity in our spiritual walk. Adopted thoughts from the enemy are the strongholds in our lives. And don't deceive yourself into thinking the Lord doesn't know what those thoughts are. Our thoughts are never done in secret.

...the Lord searches all hearts and understands
every intent of the thoughts. I Chronicles 28: 9

We talk a great deal about *the power of our choices,* but it helps to realize that the power of choice operates in our thought life more than any other place. That's why so many adults have problems. They were never trained as a child to control their thoughts. They never stopped to consider that the mind is like a sponge. Whatever a sponge absorbs is going to come out when it's squeezed, and pressures squeeze the mind.

When you are under attack begin to retrace your thoughts, and you'll be surprised at the subtle little culprits you start uncovering. Then find a scripture promise that contradicts that negative thought. Say what God says until you literally drive that negative thinking out of your mind. Say what God says until you believe it. The Word of God is a weapon that is able to judge the thoughts and intentions of the heart.

The Word of God is living and active... and able to judge the thoughts and intentions of the heart.
                                                    Hebrews 4: 12

When we control our thoughts we have just overcome **Satan's mightiest warfare weapon** and we have put those **mind vultures** to flight!

Chapter 9

Curses, Vows and Dwelling Places

I made mention in the previous chapter of how curses affect our thought life, but I could not, in all good conscience, consider this book complete without at least mentioning the importance of breaking ancestral curses. A curse is nothing more than a demon stronghold that has been handed down from one generation to the next through the family bloodline. In an overview of Deuteronomy 28: 15-68, curses fall into three main categories: sickness, extreme poverty and calamity. The world lives with, and almost boasts about curses. You have heard many of these statements: *"There has been a long history of heart disease in my family. My grandfather died of a heart attack and so did both of his brothers, and now his son has heart trouble."* Or you may have heard, *"Oh, a hot temper just runs in the family. We blow up over nothing, but we're quick to get over it."* Or perhaps, *"No matter how much money my parents and grandparents made, they were always broke."* These are curses that are common place in the world, and sadly, they are common place in the Body of Christ—only because most Christians do not know that Christ redeemed us from the curse and gave us authority over every demonic assignment.

> *Christ redeemed us from the curse of the law, having become a curse for us—for it is written, "Cursed is everyone who hangs on a tree"—in order that in Christ Jesus the blessings of Abraham might come to the Gentiles, so that we might receive the promise of the Spirit through faith.*
>
> Galatians 3: 13-14

A curse without cause does not alight. Proverbs 26:2b

Some people are shocked to hear that every demon that comes in to oppress had to come through some open door. Satan cannot just slap a curse on us because he feels inclined to do so. When it is an ancestral curse someone up the bloodline opened the door, either knowingly or unknowingly, and the results will pass down for generations until someone uses the authority that he has been given in Jesus to break the curse. Of all the doors that open one to a curse, abuse is perhaps the most unfortunate, but it, too, can be healed and the curse broken.

Disobedience is a root cause that comes from a bad tree and the curse is a fruit that comes from that bad seed. The moment Adam and Eve were lured by Satan to partake of his sinful lust the curse appeared, and immediately, he had the power to do harm to man. God did not give Satan permission. It was the entry of sin into the world that gave Satan authorization to bring in curses.

Under the Old Covenant there was no remedy for the curse; therefore, keeping the law (staying obedient to God) and looking forward to the time of redemption through the Messiah was the only protection that man had.

The curse that goes down the bloodline is of like nature to the sin itself. For example, the sin of lust and adultery in King David's life brought a curse of lust and sexual immorality on his children. The sexual immorality was obvious in his sons Amnon, Absalom and Solomon. David's sin of murder also brought a curse of murder and bloodshed on his descendants. That was obvious when Absalom had his own half brother killed. Most of the grief we see in the life of King David was over the curses that manifested in the lives of his children **that had passed down from him**.

The same enemy who tempts us waits for an open door to get to our children and our descendants; and when that happens, innocent descendants (who are not aware of the redemption that has been made available in Christ) suffer. That doesn't sound fair, but sin and Satan and the consequences of sin have never played fair; and they never will.

An iniquity curse means *a bent and leaning toward* a certain weakness. That simply means that the one suffering from a curse has a specific pull in his life toward that particular sin. Sometimes, even after being delivered from the curse, the person may still experience a tug in that area of weakness against which he has to be on constant guard until that iniquity is completely yielded to the obedience of Christ.

This is not a comprehensive chapter on explaining curses—where they come from and how they operate. The focus in this section is simply to give a practical application on how to be set free from generational bondages.

One of our biggest opportunities of rejoicing through the years has been in seeing curses lifted off of different families. I am reminded of the exasperation and helplessness that we felt when this one couple seemed to constantly be plagued with marital problems. When an argument would begin, the pattern was always the same—the wife would provoke the situation until it was out of control and then threaten to leave. Time had certainly not made things better. In fact, things had digressed until several of the encounters had ended in calls to the police station when the husband had become physically abusive during one of these emotional outbursts.

Nothing made sense! The couple appeared for the most part, to be very much in love, yet the young wife would snap at the first sign of dissension and appeared to be determined to tear down the marriage with her very own hands (mouth). Her threats of divorce would have convinced any onlooker that the marriage meant little, or nothing, to her.

On one of the occasions, however, while Jack was praying for them, the Lord spoke to him that there was a curse of rejection that had been handed down on the wife's side, obsessing her with the fear that the husband was going to leave. She saw every conflict as the one that would finally end the relationship, so the self-protection device that she chose was to get it over with, push him to the limit and ask for the divorce herself to save face. When Jack helped her to acknowledge that fear, she was more than willing to have the curse broken and submit to the counseling that taught her how to combat those thoughts and feelings of *rejection* and *fear of abandonment*. The husband was also delivered and now, a decade later, no one would suspect that this couple had ever had a serious argument. They are the epitome of a perfect family.

Another woman who came to Jack for help was in a terrified state. It was her 40th birthday, and she suddenly realized that none of her ancestors had lived past that age. After discussing it for a while, Jack was convinced that it was a *curse of death* on the family, and to his surprise, as he commanded that curse to be broken and leave her body—her eyes closed, and she turned a strange grayish color as she slipped lifelessly out of her chair onto the floor. Jack said that a barrage of mental pictures and thoughts flooded his mind: *how would he explain her death—should he call the police—had he just ended his career as a minister...?* But God impressed him to ignore what it looked like and keep commanding the family curse to release her. In a few moments, to Jack's great relief, her eyes began to flutter and color came back into her cheeks. Unlike the woman who had come through his door earlier, it was a very peaceful, happy lady who left that day. That was some fifteen years ago and we still hear, on occasion, that she is alive and doing well.

God acquainted us with information about breaking curses in a very unusual way. Soon after my first deliverance a door opened for us to be introduced to a ministry that was going to change my life even further. Someone put Frank and Ida Mae Hammond's book *Pigs in the Parlor* in my hands. This was just a short time after my first deliverance and at that time I didn't know that deliverance was an on-going process, and we knew nothing about curses. I just sensed that there was still something keeping me from being totally free, and their book gave me some knowledge about the workings of generational strongholds and spirit groupings that was invaluable.

I can remember the day that, with fear and trembling, I called the Hammonds. Their book had circulated the globe—how could I expect them to have time for me! Yet, beyond my fondest hopes or dreams, they invited me to Plainview, Texas, to a deliverance conference where I not only had further deliverance, but where a missing puzzle piece was finally brought to light. They and their deliverance partners, Pastors Jimmy and Lynda Low, explained and broke inheritance curses off our entire family.

Ida Mae Hammond kept saying to me, "The curse is coming through your *maiden* blood line," but when I told her my maiden name was *"Crow,"* she only looked puzzled. Finally, however, when my mother's maiden name *"Smith"* was mentioned, she said, "Yes, that's it!" When I thought it through, I realized that the depression had not been in my father's side of the family (the Crow side). It was Grandfather Smith on my mother's side who had a history of "blue" spells, as the old-timers called it. Depression had run in my family and God had made clear the exact bloodline curse that needed to be broken.

***

PAIN INSPIRED DECISIONS

I never cease to be amazed at the damaging decisions that I have witnessed people make through the years, simply because at some point, they were badly hurt. It is tragic to realize that one painful experience can cause someone to make a decision that produces heartache for decades to come. Obviously, those *pain inspired decisions* come straight from the enemy himself. I have never once seen good fruit come from a decision that was made based on pain.

All men are abusers. I will never again trust another man... I will steal if I have to—my family will never go hungry again... I have helped my last person. They always turn around and bite the hand that feeds them... I have been hurt for the last time. No one will ever hurt me again. Do any of those statements sound familiar? If not in your life, more than likely you have at least heard similar statements from other people. Although I am not going into detail on this subject, I will share a tragic story of a pain inspired decision made by a twelve year old child that marred his existence for the next three decades of his life.

Thankfully, there was someone who cared enough to keep him from making a decision that would have destroyed his eternity.

We first met Roger (who has since gone home to be with the Lord) when an evangelist friend of ours brought him to our home for restoration after his deliverance from homosexuality. Homosexuality is not something that one is born with; and it was our friend who put forth all the effort in helping Roger break free from that lifestyle, so I won't go into those details, but I bring up Roger's story only to relate an incident that he shared with me.

Roger said that he remembered the *exact* moment "something" entered him. Things had happened when Roger was young that caused him to hate his father. Those feelings of hate, unforgiveness, bitterness and hurt—instead of being healed—continued to grow until Roger said that he couldn't stand the sight of his father. Right after his twelfth birthday, a family member died and Roger said that he vividly remembered lying in his bed and with all the hatred one could imagine, he made the decision that he wished it had been his father and he wanted his father dead. At that very moment he said he actually felt something come into his body, and he was never the same again. Even though hate and unforgiveness affect everyone differently, Roger said it was at that exact moment that homosexual passions entered his life. And it was some thirty, tormenting years later that our friend found him on the night he was preparing to commit suicide and helped him find his way to God and a new life in Christ. Roger told me that practically every decision that he made during those thirty years evolved out of a pain that started with his father and crept into every relationship that he had thereafter.

There are people who have gone through some very painful experiences in their lifetime and no one cares more than our loving heavenly Father. Not only does He provide deliverance, but He also provides emotional healing, which allows the victim to become a new creature in Christ, able to forgive, to be healed and to lead a happy and fulfilled life in Jesus no matter how much pain there is from the past.

I recently listened to a television interview of a woman who had been raped. Her statement so perfectly describes the answer to pain inspired decisions. When asked how she felt toward her assailant, she responded, "He stole thirty minutes of my life, but I have made a decision that I will not allow him to steal one minute more by harboring hate in my heart." That is a perfect example of someone who refused to allow pain to dictate decisions that would affect the rest of her life.

SPIRITUAL HOUSEKEEPING

From time to time we find that it is advantageous, for maintaining an atmosphere of peace and harmony, to do a *spiritual house cleaning.*

We started doing this periodically after an experience I had when we were still living in town. (I share this with much trepidation because I have not wanted to sensationalize any part of the years in which we have experienced Christ's power over demons—yet, I think there is a practical lesson in what I will relate next.) Right after the departure of an emotionally disturbed, distant relative who had been staying with us, there was a different spiritual climate in our home. Our son, who would have been about five years old at the time, had just crawled into his bunk bed for an afternoon nap. I had walked into another part of the house, when suddenly, for the very first time, I experienced seeing a physical manifestation of a demon spirit. It looked like a man—unshaved, with unkept, dark hair and very evil eyes—wearing what looked like a trench-coat. He appeared just by sitting up from that area between our bed and the wall. I cannot explain how I knew it was a demonic being rather than a physical person, but somehow I knew; and before I had time to think what to do, I found myself saying, "*In Jesus' Name, you be gone!*" No sooner had those words come out my mouth, than he disappeared. I sat down to process what had just happened when Bill began screaming from his bedroom, and as I rushed in he was hollering that a man had looked at him through his window. It was the middle of the afternoon and I thought he just had a bad dream, until he said, "Mommy, a man with a raincoat looked in my window and he had a mean face." I knew he was describing what I had just seen, except by the time Bill saw it, it was no longer inside the house. The Name of Jesus had forced it to flee. That episode was a good reminder that not only does God deliver our lives, but He actually "cleans out the house."

There was another time that Jack and I both started experiencing a heaviness—almost a depression—every time we walked into the house. It dawned on us that we hadn't prayed over the home in several months so as Jack left for work that morning, he told me that he would come home early that evening for us to do some spiritual house cleaning. I arrived sooner than Jack that afternoon and as I came through the door, I realized that the heavy feeling was gone. Thinking I must have only been imagining the heaviness before, I called Jack to tell him there was no need to rush home because there was obviously not a problem. To my surprise Jack said, "I had to get something at home earlier and decided to go ahead and pray over the house while I was there." Without my knowing that had taken place, the outcome was overwhelming—just another confirmation of the importance and the difference this can make.

I am reminded of something that took place just three houses down from where we were living in town. For several years one family after another had moved into that house, each staying less than six months, and then it would be vacant again. When a friend of ours came into town looking for property to buy, we told him that he could probably get that home at a good price since the owner was desperate to find a permanent buyer.

We accompanied our friend, and the realtor unlocked the door and stood back to let us go in first. Our friend went directly into the kitchen and began taking authority in a loud voice over demons of *murder* and *violence*. Jack immediately took the startled realtor back outside and kept him busy with questions about the yard and the exterior of the house.

We found out later from our friend that the moment he stepped into the kitchen he discerned that someone had been murdered in that room. After some investigating, Jack found that years before a wife had, indeed, killed her husband in the kitchen with a butcher knife. Our friend didn't buy the house, but interestingly, the next family that moved in didn't move out like the previous buyers. It became obvious that the authority taken over the spirits in that house had cleaned it out, making it a fit place for the next owners to live.

We have also found that in addition to occupying a building (perhaps, that is why some people believe that a particular house is haunted), demon spirits will at times attach themselves to certain objects. We knew this one evangelist who collected artifacts from the many foreign countries in which he had traveled—witch doctor masks from Africa, articles of foreign worship, voodoo paraphernalia... The collection had grown to the point that he decided to open a museum to display his possessions, in spite of advice from friends who had tried to discourage the idea. It was not until a demon manifested through one of the masks right in front of him that he rid himself of his treasures.

Zodiac paraphernalia, articles that have been used in false religious rites, witch doctor masks, books on witchcraft, figurines of Buddha or other false gods... are an open door to demons and should be thrown away, even if they are simply being used for decoration.

***

I am going to end this chapter with five quick steps toward breaking a generational curse.

1. Recognize the curse and acknowledge it.
2. Don't tolerate any part of it. Want rid of the curse with every fiber of your being. As ridiculous as it sounds—some people are comfortable with the situation in which they have been living, and they are not ready to disassociate themselves from it.
3. Repent and stop any sin that is keeping the door open. Since the curse came in through the doorway of someone's sin, true repentance is the only thing that will close that door.
4. Come into covenant agreement with God concerning your situation. In other words, find scripture promises that relate to the curse you are fighting and determine to confess and believe God's Word more than you believe the thoughts and feelings associated with the curse. Realize that the promise in Galatians 3: 13, telling us that Christ redeemed us from the curse of the law, is real and powerful and true.
5. Speak the Blood of Jesus over your life and your home just as the children of Israel applied blood over their door posts.

Angelia *Ruth* Schum

The two remaining chapters in this book, written by our daughter, Angelia, are such powerful messages that I wanted to introduce her and share those teachings with you. The word *Angelia* in the Greek means *the message* and her focus in life has certainly confirmed her name. Angelia graduated from Howard Payne University and attended Oral Roberts University. Her one request of the Lord, upon commitment of her life to Him, was that she not lead a boring life. God has been faithful to answer that prayer. During college, she and her friend, Donna Stone Crow, smuggled Bibles into the underground church in China, and the summer after college she spent doing mission work in the Philippines.

Angelia and her husband, Dr. David Schum, pastor the college department at Living Word Church. They manage the Crosslines College Coffeehouse, teach weekly Bible studies, counsel with the students and take Howard Payne University mission teams into places like Ireland, San Francisco, New York, Houston, Mexico, Estonia, India, Israel, Kosovo and Guatemala.

Angelia manages Living Word Church's full power KPSM Christian radio station, as well as their KBUB Christian radio station. Angelia founded and oversees the volunteer program that has been sending weekly Bible study teams into the TYC youth prison for over eighteen years. She and her husband have an adopted daughter, Jolena, who lives in Great Falls, Montana, with her Air Force husband, Heath Adams, and their three children, Avery, Peyton and Hunter Kent.

Chapter 10

The Soulish Realm
Angelia *Ruth* Schum

Now may the God of peace Himself sanctify you entirely; and may your **spirit (pneuma)** *and* **soul (psuche)** *and* **body (soma)** *be preserved complete, without blame at the coming of our Lord Jesus Christ. (emphasis added)*   I Thessalonians 5: 23

[Editor's note: The shorter version of the Greek base nouns are used without the endings to avoid confusion for those who are not familiar with the language and to make it simpler for English readers.]

In every church there is that "one." Everyone knows which *one* we are talking about without using the name. *This* is the one who is the pitiful, hurting, needy, pathetic soul who can turn into an angry, hostile, easily offended, sharp-elbowed, controlling, manipulative, have-to-be right, never-can-be wrong individual quicker than Jekyll can turn into Hyde. Full of themselves, they are the poster children for the unstable, immature people who have been saved for a decade and it still makes you dread spending eternity with them.

On an overseas college mission trip our team became trapped by a young lady who had many *issues*. It was necessary to keep her out of certain situations in order to avoid having things fly out of her mouth. We found that the bulk of our group time was spent in resolving her problems, listening to her talk, hiding her from prospective new converts and collectively fantasizing about putting her on a plane bound for home!

If you didn't believe in deliverance for a Christian, *Janet* could make you change your mind. I've always found it amusing to go into churches that do not practice deliverance and see how they work around all the strongholds as one person's malfunctions bump into another's. One man described himself like this, "I was the one in the group everyone wanted to avoid." The shocking thing is that they know this about themselves. It is fairly easy to see how much freedom a church has by the personal victory in the lives of its members. A church full of *Janets* makes for some interesting conflicts.

I have never doubted the practical necessity of deliverance; deliverance gave me back a mother! I am eternally thankful to God that someone introduced us to deliverance—I consider it a family heritage as well as a Biblical heritage. My husband and I work with college students on a Southern Baptist campus and I have often debated those who have no understanding of the importance of deliverance and who have never seen a first hand example of a person who has been gloriously delivered.

However, I have also seen very unusual people around deliverance ministries who still have *issues* and definite things about them that aren't right in spite of their understanding of deliverance. Even though they had been repeatedly prayed over for deliverance, something wasn't budging. Something seemed to be missing. *I believe this condition to be the evidence of soulishness.* I heartily concur that *every* person needs deliverance, yet sometimes, the malfunction is in the person himself. The soul cannot be cast out; it has to be crucified. **Consequently, every good work on deliverance needs to deal with the area of the soul, as well.** I managed to miss this concept in the Word of God for years. I had been taught about demonic strongholds and fleshly carnality, but I had no comprehension of the soulish (or *psuche* as we call it) side of life.

I survived my teenage years without getting entangled into what the world would call the "bad" sins. In Sunday school they had taught me the little ditty which lists out those really BIG ones— *"I don't cuss, drink, smoke, dip or chew, nor do I go with those who do!"* There was almost an invisible scorecard that existed internally to make sure I stayed out of those on "the list." It is a general consensus that sins are subconsciously defined in terms of black or white sins. One would think that because I had escaped the deeper levels of corruption, I would have had very little guilt on my conscience. However, that wasn't so; I still felt condemned. Then one day I stumbled onto soulishness in translating the Greek.

> *For the Word of God is living and active and sharper than any two-edged sword, and piercing as far as the **division of soul** (psuche) **and spirit** (pneuma), of both joints and marrow (possibly a reference to flesh), and able to judge the thoughts and intentions of the heart. (emphasis added)*
>
> Hebrews 4: 12

Noticing from this text that the soul and the spirit were to be divided started me on a study of soulishness. Commentaries will often define soul and spirit as being the same and virtually indistinguishable (many scholars tend to interchange the definition of *soul* and *spirit*), yet the first responsibility of the Word of God here in Hebrews 4:12, is to pierce them to the point of their division. I had never before thought about their need to be divided! I felt like I had split the atom in understanding why I felt guilt and conviction. My soulish realm was intertwined with my spirit.

There are carnal, fleshly sins of the *body* (soma) that are obvious to everyone—the "really bad, colorful sins" that people write about in the *soaps.* These fleshly (soma) sins make up the category that man tends to notice more readily and scorn more heavily—adultery, stealing, lying, murder...

For if you are living according to the flesh, you must die; but if by the Spirit you are putting to death the deeds of the body (soma) you will live. Romans 8: 13

God is very vocal against these *soma* sins, and without decreasing the seriousness of them, I just want to point out that there are other categories of sin that we sometimes overlook in comparison. I actually think the category of soulish sins is more deceitful because those transgressions are just as deadly as soma sins, without being as conspicuous.

Christians tend to rate how cleaned up they are by their victory over *soma* sins of the body, however, one can be free from those outward sins and still have deep internal issues. Letting God address the soulish realm is definitely a layer in the deliverance process. If soulish sins are not mastered, they will finally expand to become obvious soma sins—the *big, fleshy ones* that everyone talks about.

For the most part we have **not** been trained to think out of the spirit (pneuma) realm. If I asked you to describe your next door neighbor, you might say something like this, *"She's a tall, slender blonde who talks a lot and keeps you laughing"*—or *"She's a shy, introverted little woman who keeps her hair pulled up in a bun."* Notice, you were describing her physical appearance (her soma) and her personality (her psuche). When we are asked to describe someone, normally the first thing we do is tell what he (she) looks like physically. Then we usually say something outstanding about their personality, but nothing about their spirit (pneuma) man.

The real you is *who you are* in the spirit (pneuma), but because our spirit man is invisible in the natural realm, the world judges according to physical appearance (soma) and according to psuche—soul (personality and intellect). We are patterned after the temple—the outer court being the body (soma), the inner court, the soul (psuche) and the Holy of Holies, the spirit (pneuma).

...which things we also speak not in words taught by human wisdom, but in those taught by the Spirit combining spiritual thoughts with spiritual words. But the natural (soulish, soma) man

does not accept the things of the Spirit of God; for they are foolishness to him, and he cannot understand them, because they are spiritually (pneuma) appraised. But he who is spiritual (pneuma) appraises all things, yet he himself is appraised by no man. 1 Corinthians 2: 13-14

When we can distinguish by saying, *"That's my psuche making that decision,"* or *"That's my soma talking,"* it can change our life. As we understand the three parts of man, we can then understand that there are different types of actions evolving from these different arenas. Make it a game to start discerning from which realm you are operating.

Some people have made every decision based on their *soma* creature comfort—food, sex, entertainment... and their soul devours the leftovers. Sensual clothing designed to excite the senses and sensual talk and actions are just tools to satisfy fleshly appetites. An entertainment diet that is strictly built to feed the soul has become a national pastime.

Magazines, talk shows and movies all capitalize on the attraction of the *soma* realm. Movie producers think they have created something exceptionally profound when they develop the *soulish* realm. It has been humorous to me to watch how a movie tends to create a romantic man with depth. If they make the leading man have substance—they portray him as a reader of fine literature or poetry or one who plays the sax. Character development gets rather repetitive as they formulate and devise the only depth Hollywood recognizes. Most people don't possess a great deal of profundity past the body realm and barely penetrate the soul. **The world does not develop the spirit man at all, because he is dead until the rebirth.** Christians, however, who have had the world as their tutor, are almost in the same category because they have never recognized the difference between their soul and spirit. The spirit man is starving to death in most people because they don't feed him. One doesn't feed what one doesn't know he has!

The world has identified itself in terms of its body. But Christians never do this! Well, maybe sometimes we forget and on occasion think like the world. In college one of my closest friends had a roommate who was that perfect blonde. Every hair seemed to know its place and her clothing was the latest seasonal line. She was the topic of discussion in many circles, partly because of one little quirk that rumored around. She would spend three hours each morning in the bathroom grooming herself, which made it difficult on the other three girls who shared the living space. She never lacked for a date; however, there was an interesting phenomenon. She would go out once, sometimes twice, but never over three dates with the same young man. Her inner circle of friends was perplexed over this. Even the young men themselves could not explain why they would lose interest. She was slender and attractive, but there didn't seem to be anything deeper than hair and nails. In spite of the fact that she was a Christian, her identity was in the body (soma) realm. Although everything on the outside was perfect, people become bored with one realm. Now, years later, she is still attractive, starved for male companionship, never-married and frustrated to this day.

I remember a very handsome young man I dated (not nearly as wonderful or handsome as my husband), and he and I shared much common ground in the way of our faith. His body was his temple, but not just in the spiritual sense. I would catch him staring at his shaved, muscled arms and legs. It was quite humorous when he passed a mirror, and I realized that *we both* enjoyed looking at him when I was with him. Our relationship became serious enough that he proposed, and I'll never forget what came out of my mouth, "I can't marry you, it would create a triangle." He replied defensively, "I'm not cheating on you. There is no one else!" After repeated badgering, he would not let it go until I explained my remark, "You are so wrapped up in yourself. I would make it a threesome." At that time I was known for being subdued and for never speaking my mind, so it shocked me that something I had never admitted to myself came out of my mouth. Sadly, he never found anyone else through the years, and we kept in touch as he frustratingly tried relationship after relationship. Being caught up in just the soma realm leaves one hungering for something more.

Where is your identity? While a *soma* person is caught up in himself, a soulish person loves the world and the things in the world. (The soulish individual is motivated by one of two realms.) The first category of soulishness is *emotional*. This individual is personality driven. His entire identity centers on the *psuche*. Art, music, literature, food, beauty... simply ravish his soul. In college, his major is built around the electives and he usually never finishes his degree. There is an innate moodiness that surrounds him in low moments, and ecstasy goes over the top in his exuberant moments. When he's down, he enjoys being sad and hibernates in his room and plays heartbreaking music. At other times he is the flamboyant entertainer who jokes, calls names, goofs off and picks up random identities. He watches television to see what his favorite character is wearing. This individual categorizes life in only two terms— what is "fun" and what is "not fun." His mouth is usually open and he loves to hear himself talk. He craves affection and moves from relationship to relationship. He hates being alone. There have been few gaps between the girl he dated in kindergarten, the one who followed next and the girl he's with now. There may have even been a few overlaps! Crisis is a normal part of his life and drama is center-stage of each crisis.

It is no less soulish to be the second type. The analytical personality is like a human calculator who spits out the facts. This is the person who knows the price of cheese by the ounce when he (she) is in the grocery store. His (her) major in college is much more serious than the personality driven individual. He has a double major, specializing in the more *concrete* fields such as accounting, science, engineering, marketing... He is compulsively organized, loves rules and regulations for the "other guy" and wigs out if he loses control in any area of his life. He is the guy on the hall who continually shouts, "Be quiet, I'm trying to study!"—and isn't ashamed of it. When he watches television it is news and market trends. This is the man who prides himself with his intellect and superior knowledge. His mind runs on wide open. If it isn't *logical*, he doesn't go there. However, the *irreverent* intrigues him in the name of intellectualism. In his early years he had very few relationships, but those have been long term with ridiculously extended dating years; and if it ends in matrimony, it is because she asked him. He doesn't have crises, he creates them.

If a person is **dominated by his soul** and he (she) considers himself (herself) to be a good Christian, he often mixes his soul and spirit. Two individuals can be sitting on the same pew, listening to the same sermon, while one listens with his soul and one with his spirit. **The first one hears with his intellect.** He is impressed with the depth of the teaching. He is even more impressed with his own mind and how spiritually adept he is. He loves to argue and speculate as he mentally freewheels. He feels that what is being taught is *for everyone else.* He is highly opinionated and never realizes that his ministry was self appointed. This is a soulish *psuche* Christian.

The second man **hears with his heart**. He lets the word wash over him, and worship explodes inside of him. His spirit jumps with excitement over truth, no matter how much that truth deals a direct blow to his doctrine and preconceived ideas. He is eager to share what has meant so much to him. He lets the word he hears change his mind and he applies it to his life. A ministry evolves without his ever realizing it. This man is a spirit-led *pneuma* man.

When a Christian mixes soul and spirit, self-depreciation is often masked by a false humility. This one is tricky in theory, but easy to recognize by the way it affects the listener. I recently heard a testimony in which a young, zealous, college student made a great many self disparaging remarks. It was apparently an attempt at humility, but it just didn't set right. The audience even groaned as the self battering made its crescendo in one final remark, "I wish this tragedy had happened to me instead of you." The testimony had a confusing "spiritual sound" to it, but it brought a lurch in my stomach, and listeners, instead of being blessed, found themselves embarrassed by the remarks. Whether a person thinks too highly of himself or thinks the opposite and puts himself down—either extreme is self-focused and soulish.

From what do you need deliverance? What does the Word of God need to pierce? That thing that you are begging, with everything in you, for God to take out of you, and at the same time begging God with everything in you, to let you keep! Both are cries from inside—a *mixture* of soul and spirit. A cry from the heart is warring with a cry from the soul.

If two people form a relationship established solely on the physical, it is not hard to imagine where that will lead. However, relationships founded on two *souls* merging create interesting and often damaging soulish quagmires. In college ministry, we witness many breakups and the differences are quite remarkable. When two people are *overly involved physically,* often the breakups are bitter, destructive and devastating to the point they leave very few good memories.

Soulish breakups, on the other hand, are often moody, distractive and frequently surrounded by drama. One young man asked how I knew that he and his girlfriend were physically involved. I replied, "Physical relationships tend to have physically bitter breakups." (Sexually based relationships frequently get vicious when they part.) However, those who have kept the *spirit realm* as the priority, with body and soul playing supportive roles, it is amazing to see the integrity, the friendship and the desire for the other's well-being left permanently intact.

In immoral relationships, deliverance must be factored in to gain victory over the spiritual transfers that have taken place. Soulish links are very dangerous when seduction and lust wreak havoc with lives. Marriage should never be entered into where there are unbroken soul ties with past partners. We have discipled person after person who was experiencing a rough time in a marriage when an old flame *just happened* to contact them on the day they were most susceptible. Unbroken soul ties are like a magnet in the spiritual realm for two spirits to link at a vulnerable moment. I'll never forget the shock when this married person shared with me —"It was supernatural; John called *just when I was needing someone the most.*" It was supernatural, all right, but from a different kingdom. That magnet is what has to be delivered out of the individual.

After deliverance there are still soulish links to get rid of—old love letters, pictures and gifts from immoral relationships, certain songs that link one to the world or to an ungodly relationship, etc. The body got you into the problem, now the body has to do the right thing and put away all the ties. Then the *psuche* part of man that has been flirting with the world and focusing primarily on self has to surrender his will—heart and soul to the Lord.

Soulishness is as old as the fall. Do a study of Biblical characters and see how much *psuche* dominated their lives—men and women like Absalom, Solomon, Esau, Saul, David's wife—Michal, Samson, Lot's daughters and so on...

The psuche (soul) is both *intellectual* and *emotional*. Even King David, who loved God with all of his heart, was at times governed by his soul (psuche), both intellectually and emotionally. It was an *intellectual* decision made with his psuche that caused him to number the people to see how militarily strong he was (2 Samuel 24: 1). Then it was an *emotional* decision made with his psuche that caused him to take another man's wife and have the husband killed (2 Samuel 11). David had forgotten the (pneuma) line that he wrote, "*The Lord is my Shepherd, I shall not want...*" when he saw Bathsheba. David's soulishness led to one, actually two, of the *big* (soma) sins!

King David must have produced some good looking children. He had been known by his handsome, ruddy looks, and the apple must not have fallen too far from the tree with his son, Absalom. Absalom is a man who demonstrates how a person can be totally known by his body and his soul, but not his spirit. Absalom was distinguished by his *soma*. He must have been something to look at—the writer of Samuel himself seemed impressed!

Now in Israel was no one as handsome as Absalom, so highly praised; from the sole of his foot to the crown of his head there was no defect in him. When he cut the hair of his head (and it was at the end of

every year that he cut it, for it was heavy on him...),
he weighted the hair of his head at 200 shekels by
the king's weight.   2 Samuel 14:25

Then Absalom became corrupted in his soulish realm. He would stand by the gates of the city and compare himself to his father David, pointing out his father's faults, and promising what a better king he would make. 2 Samuel 15:5-6 points out what a charmer he was. He would touch those who prostrated themselves before him and kiss them on the hand—and the Bible says that he stole away the hearts of the men. Charm is deceitful, and Absalom was full of it. When one is full of opinions and uses his charm, his reasoning, his seductive persuasion... to accomplish his own selfish plans, those are sins of the soul that open doors to demonic spirits; and the lives involved often have tragic ends.

David, too, was known for his compelling soulish side. He had great popularity among the common people. And there is nothing as sensationally soulish as a good looking musician. The women must have flocked to the men in this family. It was once said, *"What parents do in moderation, children do in excess."* David had eight wives; Solomon's count went off the charts.

If there was an award given for the most soulish book in the entire Bible, it would have to be

Ecclesiastes. King Solomon turned out to be a soul (psuche) man, and that soulishness manifested increasingly as he neared the end of his life. The book is all about *self*—how *self* feels, what *self* wants, how terrible the world is to *self*...

I started a list of soulishness on my computer screen, and it was so convicting that I couldn't teach this principle for several years because I felt I would have my picture posted on judgment day as the embodiment of *hypocrite*. However, there is a principle to preaching yourself free, and when I started teaching on the *psuche* areas, college students have often said that these are some of the most valuable lessons they have learned. The discovery of soulishness explained why I felt like I was doing something wrong in my walk with God, even though I couldn't put my finger on any obvious, outward sin.

Soulishness creates a very unstable Christian. Man tends to concentrate on *soma* (body) sins, but the day he sees the magnitude of *psuche* sins in himself, he is horrified. When I researched the number of times the Greek word *psuche* is used in scripture, I became shockingly aware of how often the Bible addresses the area of our soulishness.

And he who does not take his cross and follow after Me is not worthy of Me. He who has found his life (psuche) (soul) shall lose it, and he who has lost his life (psuche) for My sake shall find it.

Matthew 10: 38

It was obvious to me that God wanted the soulishness in my life crucified. Personally, I worried that there would be nothing left of me if I let go of soulishness. Yet, it had proven time and time again that in the areas where I tried to chase after soulishness, I had lost what I was really wanting, but when I walked away from it, I actually gained the very thing that I needed and truly desired.

Some preach Christianity as a *self-improvement program*—a means of just producing a *better version* of "you," but Jesus told us that our psuche must *be crucified*, not just improved. Six times in various forms in the gospels we are told that if we try to gain our psuche we will lose it, but if we lose it for the sake of Christ, we will gain it.

For the most part, the body focuses on self, the soul focuses on the world and the spirit focuses on God. My dad tells a story that happened years ago about two people who incessantly complained about the temperature in the Sunday service. One declared that it was unbelievably hot in the sanctuary. The other one pulled him aside and said, "The room is unbearably cold." Not knowing how to please either or both of them, he began to ask other people what they thought. From his unofficial survey, he noticed one striking difference. Those who were hungry for God, worshippers, and strong soul winners looked puzzled and said they didn't notice the temperature. It was a glaring distinction that showed, even among church people, the discrepancy of focus. But it illustrates an important truth. The Bible clearly says *"if we walk in the spirit, we won't carry out the desires of the flesh."*

Any deliverance minister will tell you that many people do not maintain their deliverance. Jesus Himself states that those who do not take personal responsibility for maintenance grow continually worse; they become those in the church that cause problems, become terrors in ministry situations and generally give non-believers the notion that Christians have no more victory than they do!

There are people who have been prayed over for deliverance many times, but have serious soulish strongholds. Soul tries to mimic spirit and it is necessary to divide them. Identifying and diagnosing soulishness takes a large amount of explanation because it has complex layers, yet **the answer is short**—the *psuche* has to be lost to be gained. Soulishness could be discussed indefinitely; however *one cannot defeat selfishness* *by staring at it.* If we love God with everything in us, the other entities of soul and body will take their Biblical position as followers. However, if we don't pursue God fervently, body and soul will compete to become the commanders and chiefs.

Deliverance *has* to be followed up by having the soul submit to the spirit. This is the reason why many people who have experienced genuine deliverance have stopped with what God has done for them and never continued with what they have to do for themselves in maintaining it. Deliverance is God's part—this chapter outlines our part!

Chapter 11

The Truth Will Set You Free!
Angelia *Ruth* Schum

...and you shall know the truth, and the truth shall make you free.   John 8: 32

Freedom comes from knowing the truth.   Let's begin with the last word in this verse. We don't want to overlook the fact that this verse says that the truth will make you *free*.   Freedom to me means no struggle, and there are some things in my life where God has totally laid an ax to the roots and I am free in those areas.   There's so little real freedom in people, even in the church world today, yet there is so much to be said for truly being free.

Think about being *truly free* for a minute. Many of the books in the Christian market on addictions are self-help books that take the same approach as Alcoholic Anonymous.   Recently, I read a book about an author's personal struggle with pornography and his answer to this addiction. He was portraying the tragic personal lives of the women who are trapped in this industry.   He was well researched in diagnosing the condition and how pornography freezes the images into the person's mind. I couldn't wait to get to the last chapter to see how he became free! But when I came to the end of his book, the answer was his ability to keep a tighter guard on himself. He became his own zookeeper. When he had to be out of town on a business trip, he had a friend call to check up on him, and he handed the friend his hotel receipts for accountability. He stated that he would never be totally free and that he would always have to deal with the old images that tried to come back into his mind. Upon finishing the book I said, *"Where is the victory? Where is freedom in all of that?"*

In our college group, one young man's solution was "cutting the cord to the computer." If that were the only way to keep from partaking of pornography, I would say, *"Cut the cord,"* but the danger is that there is more than one computer in the world! That may be an initial, radical step, but people aren't going to like it when he comes to visit. This kind of freedom should move from the *external cords* to *internal liberation*.

There may be a struggle for a period of time while the mind is being renewed by the Word, but that renewal process should not last forever. Just because one was once an alcoholic does not mean that one will always be an alcoholic. I call the idea of always being in a constant struggle to maintain deliverance the *Vietnam** approach. You talk to those Vietnam veterans and it is unclear to them whether they ever won the war. I have had some *Vietnam deliverances* in my life where I stay in constant conflict—fighting the compulsion daily in an attempt to hang onto that semblance of freedom—but in reality, the battle is never over. That is a Vietnam deliverance!

However, there is another type of deliverance that I call the *World War II deliverance.* I like this one. Hitler is dead! Germany is being rebuilt! Japan has surrendered! This is that area in your life where you draw a line, and God separates you from that sin, and it is a totally *done deal.* The desire is completely gone. It is a place where nothing in you wants to go back to that old sin—where there is nothing back in *Egypt* that you want. That is the state to which true deliverance should ultimately take a person. There is a difference between being *better* and being *free*!

Real freedom is when the struggle has ceased. There are some areas of sin that have never been a temptation to you. God's kind of deliverance can be like that category—an area that no longer has a magnetic pull. Have you noticed that there are

---

* I am supportive of our Vietnam soldiers and appreciative of their sacrifices and courage.

some things that just don't tempt you? You have probably never been tempted to steal camels, but I'm sure that might be a temptation to someone who lives in the desert! True deliverance should make that old struggle as much of a dead issue to you as the temptation to steal camels. It is an obvious World War II victory when a line is drawn and there is no struggle inside of you—no compelling attraction. You can be around the nicotine smoke or see the beer ads and it no longer has a pull on you.

...for he who has died is freed from sin. Romans 6: 7

There is a lot to be said for being dead. Dead people do not get tempted and they do not sin. Paul gave us a great example of true freedom when he said that we are *dead* to sin. We need to realize that there is something that happens in the spiritual realm when we become dead to certain issues. It is a place where we can stand up and say, *"I once was an alcoholic, but I am no longer an alcoholic—I'm free because of deliverance through Christ Jesus!"* Or—*"I once was addicted to lying, lust, stealing... but the addiction is gone!"* There are a great many people who are still in their *Vietnam deliverance* and God wants them to move over into their *World War II deliverance* where the battle is unmistakably won.

This might be a little more easily understood if I put it in another realm. I minister in a prison. Let's say that a "serial killer" gets saved in jail, delivered from his addiction and set free. Several months later you go back to check on his progress and he says, "Man, I'm doing great. I used to murder several people every week, but I've cut it back to only one a week. " What kind of freedom is that? It would be hard to label some areas of partial deliverance as an improvement! I've had my share of cutting-back areas!

When you ask some people how they are doing in their struggle against fear—or anger—or lust— and they say, "*Oh, I'm better,*" I want to make one thing clear—**there is a difference between being better and being free.** Raise your faith level to see that "better is better," but "free is free!" I'm glad for "better"—but better does not compare to "free."

> ... *on the first day of the week, He first appeared to Mary Magdalene, from whom He had cast out seven demons.*   *Mark 16: 9*

Many churches today never take the Mary Magdalenes through deliverance—so the Mary Magdalenes just cope. Jesus personally took her through deliverance. It amazes me that the Bible recorded even the number of demons that tormented her. Can you imagine Jesus personally taking you through deliverance? Most anyone who meditates on this scripture never questions deliverance again.

"Is deliverance for Christians or is it just for non-Christians?" Why do we ask questions that Jesus didn't ask? He never went up to a person and asked—*"Are you a believer?"* If He saw a demon, He cast it out. It's simple. Don't make it complicated. We need to follow His example. If there is a demonic struggle in our life, we just need to get rid of it—and deliverance is the method that God provided to accomplish that. Mary Magdalene actually went through a very personal, thorough deliverance. As a result of the conventional church's failure to take their Mary Magdalenes through deliverance, twenty years later they are still trying to suppress their demons.

Christians tend to get in the mode of *making their demons behave.* That is comparable to having a beach ball that you have pushed under the water. With effort you can hold it under, but there are times that the ball will slip out of your hands and come flying out of the water. Demons behave in a similar manner. We can control demons to a certain extent, but there are times that they pop up at just the wrong moment. David soothed Saul's demons with a harp. That lets us know that there are some things that you can do to soothe a demon;

Saul's servants would call on David whenever Saul's bout with an evil spirit became unbearable.

Saul would get relief as David played, but he never got free. We've all known people who live in homes where they are cast in this *harp-playing-demon-soothing* role. Perhaps, there is a *rage-aholic* in the home, much like Saul, and the best music and the best food are given like peace offerings to temporarily satisfy them.

Many young people today are filled with pain, and I believe that some of the loud music is being played to soothe and drown out the memories, the voices, the torment and the painful thoughts—to help them cope. I call certain styles of music *coping music*. Much of what we do is cope instead of getting set free. Our coping mechanisms may make us better, but they will never make us free.

What is it that is determining the very course of your life? It may be an area where you look good on the surface because you are keeping your demons under cover, but deep down you are struggling to maintain a superficial calm. We need to ask ourselves, *"What do I have hidden below the surface that pops up from time to time?"*

John 8:32 says, *"...and you shall know the truth, and the **truth** shall make you free."* We have looked at the quality of freedom, but now let's take a look at the first part of this verse—the concept of *truth*. Could the church be receiving only the degree of freedom that is in direct proportion to the degree of truth that she has? Now make that question more personal. Where are you struggling? Could you only be as free as you have allowed truth to do its work in you?

Many people have come to the place of confessing that they have been abused, and admitting that secret does bring a certain degree of freedom, but very few have come to the place of confessing that they were the abuser. I shall never forget listening to a testimony in which a young lady testified to the abuse that had come to her because of the iniquity curse that was on her family. She went on, however, to admit that because she was older she bore the most responsibility. In seconds she had transitioned from being a victim to that of being a victimizer. For a moment the congregation was stunned, however, as the impact of what she said settled over the crowd—they realized that it wasn't the kind of cheap confession you find in some convenience store novel. It was a powerful act of faith that had the capability of setting other people free, as well. Courage went through the audience because of her deep love of truth. Suddenly, the altar filled with people who were moved to repent, confess their sins and receive prayer. In an instant, I saw the church transition from the healing of victims like we've witnessed in the last couple of decades—to something I had never seen before—an altar filled with victimizers being set free. For one week people continued to come, confess and seek prayer.

Are you free? Has truth done a work in you? I challenge you to a deeper level of truth.

Reality versus Truth

*...those who perish, because they did not receive **the love of the truth** so as to be saved.*
(emphasis added)   2 Thessalonians 2: 10

If I were going to divide a congregation into two groups (authentic Christians and those who are on dangerous ground) based on the criteria in this verse—the Biblical basis for distinction seems to rest on whether one is a *lover of truth.* Often times sitting side by side on a church pew is one who loves truth and one who avoids truth. Both groups are in churches today, yet there is a fundamental difference in the outcome of their lives.

Notice this scripture doesn't say that there are people who do not receive truth. It says that there are those who do not receive the "*love*" of truth—

"so as to be saved." Interestingly, Paul is indicating that the love of truth is in direct relationship to one's salvation. In fact, Revelation 22:15 makes the same point from the opposite perspective. It says that the ones who go to hell are the *ones who love and practice lying.* The Word of God draws a vast dividing line between "lovers of truth" and "lovers of lying"—and to be on the wrong side of that dividing line is of eternal consequence. When a person doesn't receive the love of truth that is being offered by God, 2 Thessalonians 2:11 tells us that a *deluding influence comes upon him so that he believes what is false.* When that deluding influence comes on a person, lies and liars will suddenly become attracted to him—then he starts getting and giving wrong information. It is frightening to realize that one can come to a point of rejecting the love of truth until he blurs the difference between truth and deception. One's walk with God can actually be measured by how quickly he runs to truth—and how much he truly loves truth.

I told one zealous young man who was an aspiring preacher, "You will have to first learn to *tell* the truth before you can *preach* the truth." There has to be truth going *into* us, as well as truth coming *out* of us at all times. In the pew, behind the pulpit and in our own private lives we need to search to see if we truly *love* truth.

If you have an area where things consistently go wrong, look closely and you will often find that there is not an adamant love of truth because truth always sets one free. Just to *acknowledge* truth is not enough; man will not continue to adhere to the truth unless he chooses to love it.

As an individual we need to ask ourselves, *"Do I really love truth—or do I justify? ...take liberties? ...make excuses? ...cover over certain gray areas?"* Some people will go as far as finding some scripture to hide behind to defend questionable ideas and actions. Manipulating scripture is a dangerous ground spiritually.

What are some things that cloud one's perception? Half truths can be equally as harmful as a lie. If someone with marital problems comes in for counseling and tells only his (her) side of the story without telling what he did to provoke the problems, he has no real love of the truth and no real desire to have the marriage healed. Even if his part is just ten percent of the problem, it is amazing what ten percent can do to change the entire direction of a story. For example, the wife tearfully confides, "I cannot believe my husband had such a fit of anger that he actually broke out the window." From that statement it sounds as though the woman has to endure this husband who has unprovoked temper fits, until you hear that the reason he broke the window was because the wife had locked him out of the house. She omits one little detail—that the husband accidentally broke the window while trying to open the lock. Then the wife retorts "It was your two year old son who shut the door and I didn't know it locked!" ...and so it goes. Too often the partners refuse to give one shred of evidence that favors the other one, as if they enjoy seeing how few facts they can be forced to admit. Case after case has proven that just one minor detail left out is a sign that there is no real love of truth. What a pleasant surprise to see someone in love with the truth who volunteers his own shortcomings.

A lover of truth is willing to take responsibility—"This is what I did!"—with no excuses or diversions. *Implied* lying is an art form in many circles today, yet it has its roots in Biblical days, as well. The woman at the well in John 4:17 tried to leave the wrong impression about her personal life when she answered Jesus, "I have no husband." A very pitiful "*I sleep alone*" implication came out of her mouth that she hoped would be passed over without any further questions. But Jesus cut through the smokescreen she had put around her life, "You said that right, you've had five, and the one you now have isn't your husband!" This, in turn, caused her to bring the people of her village to see the Messiah *because He told her truth* (John 4: 29). It might be uncomfortable at first, but people are starved for truth and they like the way it feels when they get it out. It amuses me to watch college students catch each other on this. They will cry out a hearty, "*Smokescreen! Smokescreen!*"—until the person has to bring himself into accountability and search for truth.

There seems to be a dramatic shift among the younger generation toward honesty. People in commercial marketing say that this younger generation demands authenticity. I have been amazed at how willingly many of the young believers today will admit to something that is detrimental to their reputation, exposing their vulnerability simply because of their love for truth (note the testimonies in the back of this book). I have seen bondages break instantly in the moment of truth.

Remember, demons fear exposure; and people who are oppressed by demons have the same nature. When someone gets close to something that a person is concealing, it is amazing to what great lengths they will go to cover their secret further. The person who needs deliverance the most will often run in the opposite direction. Recently, I happened upon someone at the store who had been out of college Bible study for a while. When asked where she had been, she replied, "Ever since some things surfaced from my past, I've been running from everything connected to God." Recognize *that impulse to run* as the enemy's fear of exposure. He knows if he is found out, he will be cast out.

Freedom starts at the point of truth—not necessarily at the point of prayer—or even at the point of seeking help. Freedom starts when you look at yourself and decide, "*I am going to tell myself the truth.*" If we are content with surrounding ourselves with smokescreens—there is no real love of truth in us. Some of the worst mistakes I have made in life were the times when I was not honest with myself. And sometimes being truthful with ourselves is harder to do than one might think.

> *Every man's way is right in his own eyes.*
> Proverbs 21: 2

Not everything you *hear* on the inside is truth. Not everything you *feel* is truth. Even though Elijah was a prophet, not every voice <u>inside</u> of Elijah was truth. He stated that he was the only one left serving God (I Kings 19: 14-18), but God said, "*Elijah, your math is wrong. You say there is only one. I say there are 7000.*" It is possible to have a prophetic gift on your life, and at the same time, not be telling yourself the truth.

In Daniel 4:34, Nebuchadnezzar returned to his right mind when he told *himself* the truth. Truth brings us into a right mind. There is not a more worthwhile pursuit than that of desiring a compass on the inside that reads a true *north*. History has proved that any motive other than a love of the truth will degenerate. In fact, practically every problem that has ever happened in the life of an individual, in the life of a church or even in a nation started from a lack of the love of truth. When there is not a real love of truth— Romans 1: 25 tells us that the world degenerates until it *exchanges the truth of God for a lie.*

Let's examine the level of truth working in our lives. Truth is not contained in the mind. It goes deeper than the intellect. In some ways we think of deliverance as mental and we seek to understand it before we'll experience it, but deliverance and truth pierce through the analytical mind. Let me illustrate this concept. Not too long ago, Pastor Jimmy Low prayed for me for deliverance. It is difficult to put in words what took place, but the truth of what was spoken and the freedom it brought went past my mind and did a work in my heart. I walked out completely different, and I can't tell you why. What Pastor Low spoke by the Holy Spirit operated deeper than mental comprehension. The mind has to be renewed to truth, but don't limit the work of truth to just a mental change. **The truth comes into the mind, clears it up and gives you that burst of clarity, but then it travels to the heart and changes the life.** This is where it does its best and deepest work.

Honesty and truth are often considered to be synonymous terms, but they need to be separated. There are three levels of clarity: (1) lying, (which we have discussed previously) (2) reality, and then (3) truth. Some people will move out of lying into reality and they think they have arrived. Reality has its place. It is definitely a big step above deception. In Luke 15:17 when the prodigal son came to his senses, he came into reality. He saw how foolish he had been and what a mess he had made of his life—*I wish I had what the pigs have (verse 16)*. For him, that reality was definitely a positive step on the road home, but reality can at other times be very harsh and very negative. For example, when Amnon awoke to the *reality* of what he had done to his half sister, Tamar, in 2 Samuel 13, he hated her and locked her out of the house. That *reality* brought hurt, not freedom. **Truth brings freedom; reality often leaves you without answers.**

The Biblical definition of truth is not "*reality.*" Many people confuse reality with truth because reality is a step closer to truth than lying, but it is still not truth. Reality is, however, the doorway that can lead into truth. But if we stop at the reality stage, it has no redemptive power. There are a great many cynical, powerless people who live in reality. Reality may say, *"I don't love my spouse anymore, therefore, I want a divorce."* This particular statement may be loaded with reality, but is totally devoid of truth. Many people have come to the reality that they have been used and abused, but that reality, instead of blessing their lives, has often done nothing more than bring bitterness to a heart. A person can be brutally honest and still be without truth and subsequent victory.

Truth tells us, *"Only a fool won't accept correction."* Both compromise and a lack of appropriate correction show a deficiency of love of the truth. Confrontation is one of the highest forms of love when one is able to say, "I love you enough that I put our relationship on the line to tell you truth that will set you free." Someone once said, *"If all of your correction comes from your enemies, that is a sign that you have no real friends."* A true friend should be the first one to tell you when you are wrong. Truth speaks to us loudly, *"Deceitful are the kisses of an enemy, but faithful are the wounds of a friend."* Accepting God's correction is a sure sign of one's *love of truth.* At first some only take truth in small doses.

Deepen your capacity to love truth in bigger proportions.

Too many people are looking for a deliverance minister who is "in tune" enough to see past our smokescreens and reveal all the things we have carefully concealed year after year. But the Bible doesn't tell us to wait to confess until someone has enough discernment to figure out our faults. **The Bible tells us to confess our faults**. The testimony I shared earlier of the young college student who made a bold stand of confessing that she had the greater responsibility because she was older caused a reaction in people. Many who had hidden similar things in their lives for fear of exposure began to face the truth.

One young man who had at one time been passionate for God had turned into an emotional mess. After he let truth do its work in him—he returned to his original fire. Truth instantly delivered him from six months of emotional fog and what some had predicted to be a permanent backslide. In another meeting, a woman came forth and repented of an affair when she heard me relate the testimonies of those in our college group who were bold with the truth. (It is not necessary to tell the whole church—or even another individual—but it is absolutely necessary to admit it to God and to one's self.) Truth does a wonderful work in the heart and mind. In whatever area you are withholding honesty is the area where you are not experiencing freedom. The love of truth will determine how quickly you will have a release and to what extent.

Let's look again at our theme verse:

...If you abide in My Word, then you are truly disciples of Mine; and you shall know the truth, and the truth shall make you free.   John 8: 31-32

The truth making us free is only a fragmented concept unless we read verse 31, which defines what truth is. It is not someone's opinion. It is not the reality of your circumstances. **A person will become only as free as the amount of God's Word that he has in his life.**

Exactly what is the difference between *truth* and *reality*? A person can admit that he is in fear and that may be a reality, but it's not truth. However, the day that person says, *"God has not given me a spirit of fear, but of power, love and a sound mind"*—**that is truth**. A person can admit that he is sick and that may be a reality, but that is not truth. But the day that person says with faith, *"By the stripes of Jesus I am healed"*—**that is truth.** So many times what we are calling truth is just reality, and reality has no power in and of itself.

You may have been lying to yourself that everything in your life is fine, and then something happens that gives you a moment of clarity and you admit, *"There are some things wrong in my life and I am about to make some of the biggest mistakes of my life. I am ready to throw it all away and there is nothing in me that really cares."* That may be reality and you may think that realization and that admission is truth, but that is not truth. Truth comes the day that you look yourself in the mirror and say with faith, *"Greater is He that is in me than he that is in the world!"*

Most of the time we teach reality as being truth, but **reality is based on this natural world.** Truth goes beyond the limits of this physical universe. The psalmist said, *"Thy Word, Oh Lord, is truth."* Jesus Himself is truth, and it is only in the power of His absolute truth that we are set free. Joel 3: 10 reads, *"Let the weak say, I am a mighty man."* **Spiritual maturity comes when we move out of *reality* into *truth*.** Facing what the world calls facts—or facing reality—is nothing compared to the power we come into, and the deliverance we receive, when we love truth and speak truth into our life.

SUMMARY

Time restraints make it impossible for us personally to take everyone who reads this book through deliverance, but because this is a day and age when the need is greater than ever, it is imperative that Christians everywhere learn how to take the authority that God has given and begin using it. Deliverance is not something that has been reserved for a *chosen few.* It is a necessity for all. Unfortunately, many Christians have stayed away from deliverance in spite of the fact that Jesus spent a large percentage of his earthly ministry casting out evil spirits. But the Word tells us in 2 Timothy 3: 1-5, *"In the last days difficult times will come."* The need for deliverance is greater than ever.

Behold, I have given you authority to tread upon serpents and scorpions, and over all the power of the enemy, and nothing shall injure you.

Luke 10:19

And these signs will accompany those who have believed: in My Name they will cast out demons, they will speak with new tongues; ...they will lay hands on the sick, and they will recover.

Mark 16: 17-18

There are those who get into strange things that aren't biblically based. If the enemy cannot keep us from using our God given authority, he will tempt us to misuse it and get into some weird doctrine. Using our authority should be patterned as closely as possible to the examples that we see in the life of Jesus. Notice that His methods were never *new age* tactics, *mind control* or *bizarre* practices.

"Not by might, nor by power, but by My Spirit,"
says the Lord.   Zechariah 4:6

If at all possible find a reputable deliverance ministry and submit yourself to its leadership with the goal of becoming an arm of that ministry to set the captives free.

***

I am going to walk you through a typical deliverance preparation. There are no hard and fast rules to go by, but these are things we have found through the years to be helpful in taking someone through deliverance.

Jesus always sent His disciples out in twos. It is a good policy to have a deliverance partner—one who operates in faith, who believes in deliverance and who will be a prayer support during the ministry time.

Be prayed up. You may also find it helpful at times to fast and to ask the one who is seeking deliverance to fast. It is also important to see that the one being prayed for sincerely wants deliverance since it is extremely hard to separate someone from his friends. The one who wants freedom as much as he wants his next breath of air is going to get the victory.

Begin your session with prayer, declaring God to be the Deliverer and thanking Him for what Jesus did on the cross to make deliverance possible. **Plead the blood of Jesus for protection over all who are present and over the place in which you are doing the deliverance.**

Explain the importance to the one being delivered to forgive anyone with whom he may have ought against and then give him time to actually forgive those individuals before you begin. Have him renounce any and all dabbling with the occult (horoscopes, ouija boards, tarot cards...) no matter how long ago the involvement may have been or how innocent it may have seemed at the time.

Pray in the Spirit for discernment and for the ability to hear God clearly. The gift of discernment will be your greatest tool. What appears to be the obvious problem may not necessarily be the main stronghold because demons often mask themselves behind other spirits.

Don't set time limits. Be prepared to stick with it until you get the victory. Encourage the one being prayed for to work with you by setting his "will" like flint against whichever spirit is being called out. Don't ask God to do the delivering and don't *pray* for the spirits to go. *You* have been given authority in Jesus' Name to *command* the demons to go.

If spirit manifestations in the one being prayed for seem to get out of hand, command the spirit to leave without tormenting. **Remember, you are the one in charge, not the demons**, so don't allow them to run the show. There may be a time when you feel the need to command the demon to identify itself in Jesus' Name. In Mark 5: 9 Jesus commanded the spirit to reveal its name, but **don't dialogue with the spirits or try to get other information from them.** Demon spirits, like their father, the devil, are all liars. You are not there to interview them.

Deliverance is like peeling the layers off an onion. With each layer that comes off, one gets freer and freer. Just as is indicated in the Lord's Prayer to pray **daily** for deliverance from evil, **it is an ongoing process—not just a one-time experience.** Sometimes God cleans up only one or two areas at a time. Perhaps, that is all the person being prayed for can stand against at the present.

Don't be afraid to start out as a novice. Every doctor has to have his first case. The majority of the people in the room who prayed for me the first time were Baptist deacons who had never before taken anyone through deliverance. In Mark 9: 38-40 John wanted Jesus to stop the person who was casting out demons because he was not being trained like the twelve, but Jesus' answer was not a discouragement to the young novice. Jesus was basically saying, "*Leave him alone. After he sees the miracles that come about in My Name, he won't easily be able to speak evil against Me.*"

Don't get under the pressure of thinking that the success of the deliverance rests solely on your shoulders. **Trust completely on the Lord to accomplish His good pleasure.** He has very unique ways of achieving what He's after. When Kari Donaldson Dingler was a student at Howard Payne University, she found herself being pulled toward deliverance while at the same time battling a great deal of skepticism and doubt about its legitimacy.

Finally, after being convinced that she needed deliverance, she reluctantly submitted herself to be prayed for—only to be attacked by every kind of doubt and uncertainty and cynicism imaginable as the deliverance started. But I never cease to be amazed at the goodness of God and the measures He is willing to take to draw us into His peace and into a deeper dimension of faith.

Kari tells in her own words what God did in an instant of time to change her life forever, *"Suddenly, I saw the manifested presence of Jesus so bright that it almost hurt my eyes. I was not able to see His face because of the light. His form and His clothing were the whitest white I had ever seen in my life—He looked almost iridescent. I had never seen anything that white before, nor have I since. I remember that His arms were outstretched as He reached for me, and what I experienced at that moment changed my life forever. All the skepticism and all the doubt instantly left my being and I just wanted to stay in His Presence and never leave. Then God did another miracle to prove that He was right there with me and to confirm that deliverance was real and was, indeed, His will for my life. Pastor Ruth began calling out spirits with such discernment that I knew the entire thing was supernatural. He called out things that would have been impossible for him to have known in the natural."* Kari's deliverance is just one of many that God used to confirm not only His Presence, but also His desire to see people set free.

***

As a rule people will not readily support a deliverance ministry financially. It doesn't carry the glamour that some other ministries carry. And often a person can accept medical treatment more easily than they can accept the casting out of a demon, therefore, it's easy at times to get discouraged. You may also feel temporarily drained because deliverance is actual combat with real, live demon spirits in the spiritual realm. That is why it is vitally important for the person who operates in a ministry of deliverance to be continually filled with the Spirit by spending time in God's Presence, in His Word and in fellowship with other believers. Not everyone will agree with the ministry of deliverance because it definitely takes one out of his comfort zone. 2 Timothy 3:5 talks about *those who hold to a form of godliness, but deny the power.* Don't allow another person's denial to intimidate you or cause you to back off. In the end, nothing is more rewarding. There is no greater thrill than to know that you have been used by God to help set the captives free.

Matt and Sonda McGowen

My testimony begins like so many others... I grew up in a Christian environment and was exposed to the truth of the Gospel. Early on I had a good grasp of the *facts* of the Gospel—I knew that Jesus Christ is the Son of God, had died on a cross for us, was resurrected and promised to return. But like so many people, young and old, I did not understand how that truth was relevant to my daily life. "What difference does all this Christianity stuff make to normal, everyday living?" If anyone ever answered that question for me, I missed it.

Being raised with some exposure to church, and being a part of a family with solid biblical values, I knew right from wrong. But as I made my way through high school, the faith began to seem less and less relevant and as a result, my entire value system began to unravel. I either didn't understand or didn't believe that total satisfaction, completion, and fulfillment come only through a relationship with God. Since I didn't realize that such a real and fulfilling relationship with God was available, I began to look for pleasure, completion and confidence elsewhere.

When I was 15 years old, I began experimenting with drugs, beginning with alcohol. I loved the feeling that the drugs brought about, but the high I really enjoyed was all the attention I got because of my behavior. I redefined myself—I went from "goody two shoes" to "party animal" almost overnight. I wanted to be somebody, and I gave myself to being the wildest and craziest I could be. Nothing gave me real satisfaction, and my character began to be marked by frustration and anger. After I got bored with alcohol I began smoking marijuana and very soon I was snorting crystal methamphetamine. Who knows what would have come next, but in the fall of my junior year of high school, at 16 years of age, my life changed dramatically.

One Friday night, like so many other weekend nights, I was at a party. I was angry, restless and drunk. A buddy and I set off to play a prank, but what began as a "prank" snowballed into over one million dollar's worth of destruction and vandalism. We were arrested a couple of days later and sent to the Juvenile Detention Center. My family, friends and loved ones were all shocked and heartbroken. It was at this lowest point in my life, just a kid alone and scared, that I cried out to the Lord—*really* cried out to Him. I had already been speaking to Him a lot—begging for "mercy," making promises and trying to convince myself that I would get away with this and no one would ever know.

During these longest 48 hours of my life, totally alone in JDC, I cried out to God with more than purely selfish motives. I began to realize how much I had hurt everyone; I couldn't forget, for example, the sound of my mother's wailing in the next room as I had signed my confession and the handcuffs were placed on my wrists. Not only that, I began to realize that God was real and present with me! Something was born in me then that God has been developing ever since. I had for so long wanted to be something in everyone else's eyes and had been so concerned with people's opinion of me, but God began the work of setting me free of that. He began to show me that I'd always been something in His eyes. To sum it up, through the grace of God, my focus began to turn from myself and toward the living God. After those 48 hours, I was released to my home to remain under the watch of my parents until trial (something my lawyer had said was less likely than getting struck by lightning). After three intense months I did go to trial, however, where I was sentenced to a minimum length of stay of one year in the Texas Youth Commission (TYC).

It would be impossible to list all the miracles that occurred during this time or to name all the people God used to minister to my family and me. Before going to trial and then TYC, my parents literally forced the Word of God into me. It was an extremely painful time and the change came about little by little. Also during this three-month period between crime and punishment, a little church invited my hurting family to visit. They welcomed us, broken and confused as we were. They showed me the love of Jesus in such a real, honest and tangible way and demonstrated unconditional love and acceptance. It was in that church family that I gave my life fully to the Lord and it was there that I heard His call to the ministry. That church body prayed faithfully for me during that transition time, and all the way through my year of incarceration.

At the TYC Center the Lord continued to show Himself faithful, protecting me and giving me favor. He consistently placed the right people in my path. One example of God's faithfulness is the prayer time He allowed me to have. I was incarcerated on a dorm with 24 other young men with absolutely no privacy because the building was designed for everything—bunks, bathrooms and free area—to be in the open. The only enclosed room was the group room where we met with our case-worker each day. I spent the hour each morning between waking up and going to breakfast in that loud building studying the Word and praying. After a few months, a correctional officer made the rule that I could go into the group room alone each morning for an hour of prayer and study! This time with God changed my life. Another example of God's favor is that He allowed me to begin taking classes at Howard Payne University "BEFORE" being released from TYC! Two months before my scheduled release, TYC began transporting me four hours a day, three days a week to the HPU campus where I took nine university credit hours. I was transported to and from the HPU campus in the TYC prison van, wearing my orange TYC uniform, but for twelve hours a week I was in the free world beginning my education. I graduated from Howard Payne University three years later with a Bachelor's degree in Christian Studies. What should have cost me a year of my life actually set me ahead a year in my education. God is so amazing!

That year was tough. I was separated from everyone and everything I knew and I was extremely lonely. But during that time the Lord and I developed a relationship that only someone who spends time alone can understand. He comforted me and taught me to rest in Him and to be fulfilled in Him. His became the favor and opinion I sought, and I began to define myself as a child of God. He gave me so many opportunities and sent so many people my way, but the number one thing I learned in TYC was how to trust God. All this happened little by little, a day at a time. Meanwhile, there were countless people investing time in prayer for me and writing letters of encouragement. God's people showed me Jesus Christ in real, tangible ways.

When I returned home, that little church I mentioned earlier welcomed me with open arms. I now pastor that church—the same love and compassion is here and I feel like the most blessed man in the world for being a part of what God is doing in this part of His kingdom. God has given me a wonderful wife and too much to be thankful for to even begin to write. But I can look back to those dark days and remember that there was a time when things seemed so bleak and ruined and hopeless. But God has taken a terrible thing and brought glory from it. He is so good at that! He will do it for you. Looking back several years later, it is much easier to see God's hand moving than it was when we were in the midst of the ordeal. That's where faith comes in. I shudder at what could have happened if God had not been acknowledged in my life and in this situation. Where would I be now?

Maybe you are in a struggle or you've just come through one. Or maybe there are storm clouds on the horizon and trouble around the next bend. Whatever the case, remember that God is bigger than your mistakes and His love is stronger than your sin and mine. He is able to take your biggest mistake and use it to bring good to your life and glory to Him. There is hope, no matter where you are now. Your personal relationship with God is eternally important, but we were never meant to live this Christian life on our own. Let God's imperfect people love you and pray for you and walk through life with you. You have a future. Give this day to God and see what He will do!

***

Note from the author: Matt McGowen was delivered from alcohol and drugs. Notice in his testimony the steps he took to stay free from addictions that would have destroyed his life. Matt kept himself in a 'love walk' with the Lord, daily filled himself with the Word of God and stayed in fellowship with other Christians. He not only attended church, but began to serve others. Matt started as the Assistant Youth Pastor in his church and later was promoted to Youth Pastor. When the Senior Pastor decided to resign, he recommended Matt to fill his position. At the time that this book went to press Matt was twenty-three years old and since becoming pastor three years ago, the church has seen such an explosion in growth they are now in a building program. He is active in the Epiphany outreach in the Texas Youth Commission program, has spoken at the TYC banquet to the administration, staff and volunteers and is effectively ministering in the place where he was once incarcerated. Matt also takes youth to work in the orphanages in Mexico and his Sunday morning church service can be heard weekly on KPSM 99.3 FM Christian radio.

Many times the bondage out of which God delivers you will be the very place in which you later minister. It was difficult for Matt to go back to his community, but he has been very effective in his own hometown. The results of his ministry are already reaching out to the world.

Christopher Clayton
Ali and Claire

"For by grace are ye saved through faith; and that not of yourselves; it is a gift of God; not of works, lest any man should boast. For we are His workmanship, created in Christ Jesus unto good works, which God hath before ordained that we should walk in them." Ephesians 2: 8-10 (KJV)

I have to remember this verse daily because my flesh wants to rise up and say, "I did it!" That would be a lie. I tried to do it for almost twenty years and was completely powerless and unable to stop using intravenous methamphetamines on a daily basis. Alcohol, marijuana, cocaine, LSD, prescription drugs, opiates and hallucinate agents... I've tried them all in my search. The problem was that I didn't know exactly what I was searching for. It turned out that Jesus Christ was exactly what fit that hole I had inside of me. I tried chemical cures for a spiritual problem from the time I was 12 years old until I was 34. This, of course, did not work.

As anyone knows who struggles with drug addiction, it changes from a "want to" to a "have to." **We don't see this line in front of us and choose to step over it; rather, we look behind us, and there it was.** Satan is a clever and powerful adversary when you don't know Jesus. If Satan had shown me where I would end up before I took my first drink or hit, I would have said, "No!" If I could have caught a glimpse of the misery I would endure I would have said, "No!" 2 Corinthians 11: 14 says, "*Satan disguises himself as an angel of light.*" That is exactly how he appeared to me. My first drink felt warm and gave me courage. My first experiment with drugs made me feel power like I'd never felt flow through my veins. I felt alive and in control. Satan overplays his hand because the weapon he made prosper against me for so long turned and revealed its true nature. It beat me down so badly that I had no faith in myself, so pride and self reliance no longer existed in me. My parents tried to rear me right; therefore, I knew who Jesus Christ was, even if I didn't know Him personally. I knew that what I was doing was wrong and I knew I was spiritually sick. I became incredibly paranoid and thought the whole world was against me. I began to see the demons that rode around on my back every day. I saw them crawl out of the ground, laughing and smiling at my terror. I actually saw them. This was, to say the least, terrifying. I had no solution.

My wife left at my insistence because I thought she was conspiring against me. I was alone. I knew these demons came from Satan, and I knew I could not stand against him alone. But I felt I had no choice. I could not stop using drugs so I thought I would kill myself. That had always been my way out in the back of my mind. I had tried to overdose many times with no success. I always came back to the same life I hated. I still had enough pride that I was going to control my own destiny so I got out my rifle and placed it in my mouth, but I could not pull the trigger. No matter how hard I tried it would not budge. This was a lever action with a hair trigger and no safety, yet it never fired. My way out was no more. I had no escape. It was me and these demons.

I had crawled underneath my house to kill myself and it was pitch black, but I could still see them and hear them giggle and laugh at my misfortune. It was at that moment that I surrendered—not to those demons, but to God. All I could get out was, "Please help!" I heard flapping, but for the first time in years it wasn't demon wings that I heard. It was God's angels coming to war—coming to my aid. My sin was pride and self and until I had no faith in self I would not cry out to God. It was at that moment that David Schum's voice came back to me saying, "*Satan comes to steal, kill and destroy.*" I had a moment of clarity, and I saw how Satan had played all his cards, how I had been manipulated and how the final act of "destroy" had been about to come true.

I had received the Baptism of the Holy Spirit at age fifteen with Peggy Joyce Ruth when my mom had asked her to pray for me. God answers prayers, but I turned my back on God and on this gift. Now twenty years later I started praying in tongues as I saw those angels envelop me in their wings. I felt the presence of Almighty God under that house. For the first time in years incomprehensible love and peace and joy and happiness flooded me. I *actually* felt God's protection around me and I *actually* saw the demons scream and run in utter defeat and fear. I saw firsthand what real power and glory was and it had nothing to do with me. I understood mercy and grace and knew I did not deserve it. I knew in my heart that this was my Creator, my Lord and Deliverer, Jesus Christ. All I could do was sob, "Thank you," and pray in tongues.

I awakened later in the dirt and mud underneath the house and Satan immediately tried to steal from me. It was just another hallucination, but he could not steal the peace and love that I had felt for the first time in years. I've been to numerous treatment centers, jails, halfway houses, mental institutions and self help groups. None of them gave me peace. That is how I knew Jesus came when I finally cried out, and I gave myself to Him under my house during a full blown enemy attack. He has been with me ever since. I don't know whether it was hallucinations or if I was allowed to see into the spiritual realm, but I do know that the Lord of lords and King of kings rescued me from a place that was so much worse than death.

I picked up a whole bunch of spiritual baggage along that journey that I had to be delivered from. God sent Dr. Schum and Pastor Jimmy Low just when I needed them. Demons of paranoia, self loathing, other people loathing, low self esteem, addiction, rage, schizophrenia, selfishness and many more were cast out of me in the Name of Jesus. It worked. I went into deliverance fearful and ashamed and came out with peace and tranquility. My circumstances had not changed, however, as I was still facing prison and my wife was still gone, but I had Jesus living in my heart so I was experiencing some of the Fruit of the Spirit like love and peace.

I continue to seek God and He is always there to reveal Himself to me. Had I made a list of what I wanted God to do for me I would have shorted myself. He has blessed me so abundantly in areas and ways I could not have imagined. The two scriptures that mean the most to me are John 14: 6: Jesus said, *"I am the Way, the Truth, and the Life. No man cometh unto the Father but by Me."* and John 8: 32: *"And you shall know the Truth and the Truth shall make you free."* Jesus is the Truth and the more I get to know Him, the freer I get. Thank God He didn't give me my old life back. He gave me a new, cool life. My wife came back and we have a better relationship than I ever thought possible. I have an awesome relationship with my ten year old daughter and I am able to be the earthly father she needed for years. God has now blessed me with a new daughter who I watched be born "drug free." I have Christian friends, Christian music, a new house, job... I could go on and on. The blessings are too numerous to list. He has given me a ministry sharing the Good News with other alcoholics and drug addicts. I also speak to youth inmates in the Texas State Juvenile Penal Center in our town. It is a privilege and a duty that I take seriously because it still blows my mind that God can use a man like me. I owe Him a debt I can never repay. I take credit for none of the successes in my life. I know where my way got me and I know where God's Way is taking me. All I can say is, "Thank You, JESUS."

If you or a loved one have an addiction, the chemical is not the problem. The chemical is the solution we have chosen to the problem, but it is the wrong solution. The problem is us. Flesh is the problem. I am the problem. Satan knows this. Jesus Christ is the solution. Satan knows this and he is scared. Alcohol and drugs seem to work for a time, but if they have quit working for you—the Truth can make you free. I didn't have to clean up to come to God. Thank goodness! I came to God and He cleaned me up.

"For we wrestle not against flesh and blood, but against principalities, against powers, against the rulers of the darkness of this world, against spiritual wickedness in high places.   Ephesians 6: 12

My name is Chris Clayton and this is my story. His Name is Jesus Christ and if He can fix a broken man like me, He can fix anything. Thank you, Jesus.

Susan and Bruce Wesley
Bekah, Sarah and Micah

Have you ever been exposed?   I was in second grade and it was career day at Oak Hill Elementary. The assignment was to decide what you wanted to be when you grew up, to dress to fit that career and to make a poster. I put on one of my mom's really fancy dresses that was pink and covered with sequins and beads. My poster said, "I want to be a movie star!" We were paraded through every other class and allowed to tell our ambition. I remember at the end of the day as I changed back into my other clothes, I realized that the dress I had on was really low in the back and that I had gone all day, exposing my backside. I obviously didn't have a friend in the world to tell me. That is a good picture of my life as I grew up. When you are afraid of exposing yourself, you have secrets.

Have you ever had a big secret—the kind of secret that makes your hands sweat at the thought of exposure? I was raised with that kind of secret. And it gave birth to more secrets.

One day while I was still in elementary school I got into a heated argument on the bus with a boy named Alan who lived on my block. I didn't know him very well and he had never been to my house, but he won our argument by yelling so that everyone on the bus could hear, "Well, your mom is an alcoholic!" I was horrified. You see, he was right. My mom was an alcoholic. If he knew the secret about my life, then others surely knew! My mother's alcoholism and depression was something I wanted more than anything to keep hidden.

We did attend a church fairly regularly during this time of my life—but it seemed more like a social obligation rather than a way to know God.

There was never any talk of faith or God in my home.

Every morning I would wake up to the sound of a vacuum cleaner. My mother would obsessively clean the house so that it looked perfect—and then by the time I got home from school, she would be passed out from drinking. You see, we had the appearance of a home that was "fine," but it was clearly not fine. Over time she began to threaten to kill herself. When I was in the sixth grade my dad came to school and got me out of class because mom had called at work to tell him, "By the time you get home, I'll be dead." We raced to the house and walked in terrified that she would have shot herself. She had not, but then my dad was afraid that my mom would do something to hurt my brother and me in her pursuit of self destruction, so we drove her to San Antonio to her mother's home. She threatened all the way there to jump out of the car, so I kept my hand on the door to ensure that she wouldn't.

In 1973, my dad divorced my mother in an ugly court battle at a time when dads didn't get custody of children and mothers weren't alcoholics, yet the judge awarded my brother and me to my father. I visited my mom on weekends and holidays and even though I wanted her to be a mom, she was passed out most of the time when I was there.

I kept up the lie and learned to think fast on my feet. When half of the furniture disappeared out of our house after the divorce, I told my friends that we were remodeling. I did not want anyone to know the truth so I continued to keep up this façade of "everything is okay and I am fine!"

In 1975, I had just been elected cheerleader for the coming year and was beginning to get some attention from boys when I went to Houston to spend part of the summer with my aunt and uncle. That was tragically interrupted, however, when my dad called to say that my mother had taken a bottle of pills and killed herself. I felt destroyed. Up until then I had lived with a glimmer of hope that someday she would stop drinking, my parents would remarry and we would live happily ever after. The show to watch at that time was *Happy Days* and I remember thinking, "I just want a normal family like that."

Again, I couldn't deal with the shame of my mom's suicide so I told people she had cancer. I did not have one friend in whom I could confide the truth. I didn't have a friend who cried with me, and I felt hopeless.

That school year seemed like a blur. Most days I would just go to class and lay my head down on the desk until the bell rang. I'm sure it was only the mercy of the teachers that caused me not to fail. My dad tried to help me cope, but I remember just wanting to forget it all. Dad had begun dating a woman and by Christmas of that year they were married. I know he thought this would be the answer to all of our problems, but unfortunately, she wanted little to do with me and I resented her interfering with my relationship with my dad. She never told me anything directly. She would be sweet to my face, but then I would hear her giving my dad an earful of whatever I was doing that annoyed her. So once again, I was living this life that was a façade and we were all playing the game, but no one was happy.

My freshman year we moved to Round Rock, giving us a brand new start. Dad strongly encouraged me to be independent and to learn to take care of myself, so I began to rely heavily on my friends and boyfriends for all the love and support I needed. When you are new to a school—especially a big school—a new student is likely to gravitate to the first and most accepting group. For me, it was the kids that partied. Up until this point, I had been a fairly good kid. I didn't lie to my dad or do drugs. But that year I went wild. My skills as a liar really enabled me to do whatever I wanted and my father's tendency to encourage my "independence" only made it easier to do things I should never have done. I skipped more and more school and my idea of studying for a test was to make cheat notes. I never got caught which only reinforced the habit. I got high on the way to school and high on the way home. Then I started dating a guy who was two years older than me and I lost my virginity at 15. This unhealthy relationship became my life and he became my family. I had a God shaped hole in my life and I was trying to fill it with all these things that just didn't fit. Even though I would say, "I'm fine," I remember this gnawing in my heart that made me always somewhat unsettled. My boyfriend went off to school during my junior year, but we continued a long distance relationship.

It was during that junior year that a friend invited me to church. They were having a youth service and it was there that I first heard and understood about a God who loved me. The preacher talked about how God sent His Son to die on the cross to pay the price for our sins to be forgiven and to give us a life of purpose and meaning. I felt so lost and so in need of direction that when the preacher invited people who wanted to accept Christ to come forward, I ran to the front. I prayed to accept Christ that night and went home a different person.

God immediately began to put people in my life to teach me what it meant to follow Jesus and I began reading the Bible and praying. It was then that I began to realize that I had some hard changes to make. I could not stay in the relationship with my boyfriend and follow Christ. God began to show me about His plan for sexual purity and I became involved in a church in Austin and was baptized as a symbol of my faith in Christ.

I met Bruce my freshman year in Howard Payne University and as we started dating I sensed that this relationship was different. He treated me so kindly and God was with him. I knew Bruce was a virgin, and I knew I needed to tell him the truth about my past. My being honest could make him break up with me and the grief I felt that night still haunts me. I could barely get it out of my mouth. Even though I knew I was forgiven of the consequences of that sin, it still hurt deeply. His response to me was, "This is past—that is not you today—I love you!"

Unfortunately, however, there was so much in my past that I had never really been honest about—with myself or God—that the anger and shame began to surface. I developed a serious eating disorder called bulimia. I would binge on food and then throw up every day, and this pattern became an addiction just like the alcohol was my mother's addiction. Eating disorders are about control rather than about food. This was something I had full and complete control over. No one knew and I had much practice at keeping secrets. It is like an alcoholic and alcohol. This destructive pattern caused me so much pain; I was a Christian—I wasn't supposed to have problems like this now. I felt like I was a fake and a fraud. Here I was again—living a life that was a façade and I felt so much shame.

I had a friend named Angelia and she was the kind of person who believed in a big God who could heal and deliver. I spent some time with her and her parents and I was able to tell them everything. I had suppressed all my pain. I had denied it and it had expressed itself in bulimia. I don't really understand how all that works, but I know that when I finally got really honest with myself and with God, the healing process began. And telling someone was a breakthrough that gave me hope. Angelia and her parents took me through deliverance. They showed me the truths of God's Word that gave me hope for a different life. One of those was 2 Timothy 1: 7: "*For God did not give me a spirit of fear, but a spirit of power, of love, and of self discipline.*" God used that friendship to start His healing in my life and His healing power started from the inside out.

I found out that what you choose to believe makes a difference in how you live. Romans 12: 2: "*Do not be conformed any longer to the pattern of this world, but be transformed by the renewing of your mind. Then you will be able to test and approve what is God's good, pleasing and perfect will.*" It was not instant. There were good days and bad days, but before long the good days out numbered the bad. God delivered me from the shame and the anger that I had stuffed down, and He taught me about the power of His Word.

I am so thankful that my past does not determine my future. God is a God of hope for a better future. Bruce and I have been married 19 years. We have a strong marriage—not perfect because there are no perfect people. We have three great daughters whom we enjoy so much. I still have a lot to learn about how to be a good wife and mother, but God has always been so faithful to put so many people in my life from whom I can learn. I am so thankful that my secrets were finally exposed. My life isn't *Happy Days* or *Seventh Heaven*. It is far better, and it's real. I am so grateful for the deliverance that was made possible through Jesus.

From left, back row: Scott, Reba, daughter-in-law
Yolanda, son Dustin, grandson Dylan
From left, front row: granddaughters Shaelynn and Paige

Scott and Reba Brown

Scott and I were not reared in Christian homes so
neither of us had asked Jesus into our hearts in
the 70s while we were in high school together in
the small Texas town of Cleburne. It seemed easy
to become involved in the drug scene—after all,
everyone was doing it, or so it seemed. The drugs

made you feel like you were invincible and they dulled the pain of growing up. You felt like you were a part of the in-crowd and accepted by your peers, however, no one could know the pain that lay behind that deception. We had moved in together after I graduated in 1974, and were married in March of 1976. By this time Scott's drug habit had reeled out of control, and he had become an habitual I.V. drug user and had even started to sell drugs to support his habit.

I was more low key, never using a needle, but still smoking marijuana and drinking alcohol. However, when I became pregnant I stopped using everything, but Scott was hooked and couldn't quit. He was in too deep. He would stay awake for weeks, strung out on "speed." He finally became so angry and abusive that he caused permanent damage to my back, leg and left ear during the beatings. The only thing that kept me going was our beautiful son, Dustin, who was born January 28, 1977. We lived in hell for almost two years, until finally I gained the courage to leave and get a divorce. In the latter part of 1978, I moved to Brownwood, Texas. I had asked Scott to stay out of our lives and let us start over, so to comply with my wishes he moved to Oklahoma.

I was a functional alcoholic, working every day and drinking every night, and in 1980, I married another abusive alcoholic. We were together off and on for nine years, during which time he adopted Dustin. While working at the FMC plant from 1982 to 1985, I met Jack Ruth who was always so kind and invited me to church often. We visited, but I never surrendered my life to Christ. When I divorced again in 1989, I started drinking even more heavily and felt like my life was over. Even though I was raised as an atheist, I always believed in God. I just didn't know anything about Him or about the Bible. I did not, however, believe in the devil or demons. I just tried not to think about God and thought that as long as I didn't kill anyone I would go to heaven. I knew nothing about Jesus. People had tried to tell me, but I didn't listen.

I didn't think I needed a savior, but in June, 1990, while lying on my waterbed one night, I felt something heavy get up on the mattress. My natural mind knew it didn't feel like a person or an animal, but I called out to see who it was and felt around for the cat. The heaviness quickly moved up the bed on top of me and pushed me hard into the mattress. I could not even move my face. I felt sharp fingernails dig into my hands and a deep female voice said, "I am the viper." She continued to talk, but I was so scared I couldn't hear the rest. I began to hyperventilate and cry. I could hardly open my mouth, but from deep in my heart I cried out, "God, please help me!" Immediately there was a swooshing sound, and the heaviness was gone. I turned on the light and could hear the sound of thousands of voices cackling like chickens. In a severe panic I called a friend and then I flew out of the house in my nightgown, leaving lights blaring. It took me three days to get the courage to go back home. None of my friends were Christians, and they said I was just dreaming or drunk. But I knew how real this was and that I needed spiritual help.

I had a spirit filled uncle and aunt who had tried to tell me about the Lord and had taken me to a conference when I was fifteen. I called him and he said, "Praise the Lord, you have a demon." He told me how to read the Bible and pray and anoint the house with oil.

My spiritual journey started that night! I began to *church* hop instead of *bar* hop. A young Christian man from work who was also a youth pastor invited me to his small Baptist church. He and his wife practically adopted me, and they helped me in so many areas. It took several months, but I finally accepted Jesus Christ as my Lord and Savior. He then began to change me, delivering me from alcohol, cigarettes, and cursing. He taught me what sin is and how it was destroying my life. My son was so happy to have a sober mother. He also gave his heart to the Lord and we were baptized together in May of 1991.

In July, I decided to move to the church where I had visited many years before and where Jack Ruth was pastor. I had only been there a few Sundays when Pastor Jack spoke a "Word of Knowledge." I didn't know what that was at the time, but I knew God was speaking to me. He said, "*There is a young woman here who feels as if her life is out of control. You never had a good husband, and you never had all the children you wanted. You are at an unfulfilling job. You have lost all your friends and even some family members in order to follow Jesus. But the Lord says, "I am changing someone for you to marry. I will bless your obedience."* "

I never thought about Scott because I had not seen or heard from him for twelve years. I thought he was probably dead or in prison. But on August 17, 1991, Scott's sister called to tell me that Scott had been in a terrible accident and the doctors were not sure he would live. Scott had wanted her to ask me and Dustin to forgive him. The Lord had dealt with me when I first got saved about forgiving Scott, my parents, and others, so I told her that we had been born again and had already forgiven him. I told her we would pray for him, and I called all the churches and TBN to pray also. He had been so high on drugs and alcohol that he had fallen backwards off a six foot porch, landing on his neck and breaking the C2 and C4 vertebrae. He was about to overdose, was totally paralyzed from his neck down and his lungs were collapsing. He did, somehow, live, by the grace of God, and they drilled holes in his skull to put on a halo. He was told that his paralysis was permanent and he would never get any better. I found out later that the way some of his drug buddies tried to help him was by attempting to slip drugs to him in the hospital.

I talked to Scott one time in the next week and he still sounded like the old Scott, but he had been watching TBN, and people had been ministering to him. By this time he had been sent to a rehab center to be taught how to survive as a quadriplegic.

On August 26, Scott asked his sister to wheel him into the parking garage of the hospital and leave him there. In his desperate condition he had hit rock bottom, so in that parking garage he cried out to God, *"I have totally messed up my life, and I give it to You, just as it is!"* Then he said that immediately he felt as though he had been lifted out of the wheelchair and was looking down on his old self in the chair. He said that heat went through his body, and he was filled with the Holy Spirit and began to speak in other tongues. When his sister came out to take him back to his room, she said that he had a glow about him, and out of his eyes, he looked like an entirely different person. She said that his eyes had seemed dead before and now they were alive.

Scott's sister called to have me speak with Scott. I knew before he even told me what had happened that he was changed. Everything was different—his voice and the way he talked. Even though he was still paralyzed he was so excited he could hardly slow down enough for me to understand what he was saying. He knew he had been delivered from a twenty year drug addiction and he said that he felt totally free inside.

After that, things began to change quickly. He started to get feeling in his arms and legs. Then he started to walk and to feed himself—all things that the doctors had said would be impossible. In November of that same year, the doctors took off the halo and he was released from the hospital. It was indeed a *modern day miracle with no medical explanation.*

During those three months I had come to know that the person God wanted me to marry was Scott. It was very scary for me because things had been so bad before, but I trusted the Lord. We talked and prayed about it and decided I would pick him up at a friend's house in Oklahoma after he was released, and we would be married.

At this point Scott had still not seen his son, Dustin, for over twelve years, and he was so afraid that Dustin would be ashamed of him because of his past and the scars all over his arms from the needle tracks. But what a loving, heavenly Father we serve! The next morning when he woke up, before he was to meet with Dustin, **the scars were gone,** and he said that he had this special peace that Dustin was, indeed, going to accept him. To this day there are no visible needle marks on arms that had once been covered with scars.

God united us as a family and truly returned the years the enemy had stolen. Both of us were delivered from addictions and healed physically and emotionally. We have walked closely with the Lord since then and have been together over thirteen years now. Scott and Dustin have a very close and special relationship. We have been blessed with a beautiful daughter-in-law, two wonderful granddaughters and a fantastic grandson. Scott is completely healed and owns a carpet installation business where he works six days a week. I also have a home-based business. We are so grateful for our wonderful pastors, Jack and Peggy Joyce Ruth, and our church body. We are so blessed! Our God is so faithful.

Names have been changed in this testimony
due to the other people involved.

I grew up in a family where sexual addictions
and abuse were very common and they began at a
very young age. As early as the age of six I can
remember my step grandfather molesting me and
exposing himself to me on a regular basis. He told
me that something bad would happen to me if I
ever told anyone about what was going on. This
allowed much fear to enter my life about older men
and I set myself apart from men as much as
possible.

This molestation also brought on an unhealthy
awareness of my body. I became obsessed with my
body and became addicted to masturbation.

At age ten I was molested by an older step cousin. He would force me to perform oral sex on him and in exchange would do things to me. Around this same age my younger brother and I began looking at my uncle's pornographic magazines. And before long, we were in an unhealthy relationship that continued for many years. This just added to the many other strongholds that were a part of my life. There was such a spirit of perversion on our family that it was not uncommon for me to walk in on family members performing sexual acts on one another.

The world would say that our home situation was hopelessly impossible to break free from, but I thank God and praise Him that He is a faithful Father who saves us, delivers us and heals us from every evil thing, no matter how bad the circumstances appear to be. At the age of eighteen I gave my life to the Lord and surrendered to full time ministry. Although my heart was for the Lord there were still some struggles in my life that were holding me back. I still had sexual addictions that often seemed to come at me while I was reading my Bible and praying. I had trust issues with men and some of the most perverted men seemed to be drawn to me. Because of all this, I feared that my sexual relationship with my eventual husband would be unfulfilling.

God knows our heart and in His Goodness He positioned me under an amazing deliverance ministry and began to do His miraculous work in my life. The two deliverance pastors in my life would spend hours praying me through years and years of strongholds, as well as teaching me how to pray and take authority for myself in these areas. They not only helped me "get set free", they also taught me how to "remain" free. There are many stories I could tell of the deliverances and healings I have gone through, but there are two that really stand out to me.

The first story has to do with the kind of men that were drawn to me. It seemed that if there was a pervert or a drunk within a mile of me, I was like a magnet. I would like to have believed that it was the *light of Jesus* that was drawing them to me, but in my spirit I knew something was wrong. I had my college pastors pray over me and they cast out several spirits that drew these kinds of people to me, and I have not ever had that problem again.

The second most memorable experience was the deliverance from the addiction of masturbation. I mentioned that this problem seemed to rise up more during my devotional times with the Lord, causing so much condemnation and guilt that I felt I was constantly failing the Lord. On one occasion, as I was driving down the road, I felt this desire come over me and I asked the Lord what to do. He showed me that the desire was, in fact, a demon and I was to tell it to leave and not return. I cannot even begin to explain the relief as it left me, never to return.

The Lord is so faithful. I am now married to an amazing man who loves the Lord. We are both attending seminary and we have a very healthy marriage. The Lord has set me free from all areas of fear and sexual perversion and He has fulfilled me in every area of my life. I have shared my testimony many times and people are always amazed at what the Lord has brought me through. I have been told that they would never have known I had gone through these things if I had not told them, because I seemed so free. This is such a strong testimony of God's love and His desire to COMPLETELY liberate His children. I encourage every believer to learn—not just "to cope"—but to learn to seek God for His complete and entire deliverance and infilling. There is nothing to compare to it.

Sandi and David Brown
Zoe and Shalom

I was born on a small island outside of Taiwan in 1972. My parents were both from China. When the communists took over China in 1949, my father left his family there and came to Taiwan; he never saw them again. In fact, my grandparents, whom I had never met, were executed by the communist "Red Guards" during the Cultural Revolution in the 1950s. They were brutally beaten and left to die in an outhouse; my uncle was not allowed to retrieve their bodies for burial until a month later.

My mother was just a newborn baby when the Nationalists (the then ruling party of China) were ousted by the communists in 1949. Her parents fled China with only the clothes on their backs and their infant daughter.

My parents weren't devout Buddhists when I was little. We were Buddhists by culture. We burned incense and worshipped our ancestors during Chinese New Years and other holidays. The holidays and customs in most Asian countries are totally centered in on, and evolve around, beliefs in Buddha and pagan traditions. That was how I was brought up. That was my existence.

Since my father was nineteen years older than my mother, their marriage did not work out well. My mother had married at a young age trying to get out of the hardship her mother had brought on her family. But what she did not know is that she was jumping out of a frying pan into heaping coals.

As far back as I can remember there were lots of fights, yelling, and cursing at the house. Both my parents had hot tempers. There were a few times they even tried to harm each other physically. Several times my mother packed my two sisters and me while my father was at work and moved us back to my grandfather's house. My father would come in a week or so to beg for my mother to come back. Things would be better for a little while, but then there would be more fights and yelling. It was like a nightmare that would never end.

At a young age I was longing and searching for stability and love. For some reason I knew Buddha was not the answer. I've always disliked the temple. It was a dark and uninviting place. When I was in the fifth grade a missionary handed me a gospel tract on my way to school. I read the tract and was drawn to God's love for me that was described there. Deep in my heart I knew every word in that little booklet was true, and I simply wanted to be with God. I accepted Jesus as my Savior and prayed the prayer offered in the tract.

I was born again by the power of God through Christ, the Expression of my Father's love for me. At that time I didn't know that I needed to be in church; neither did I know where to find one. I didn't own a Bible. In fact, I had never seen one in my life. But what I did know was that I belonged to God, not Buddha. I would talk to my friends about God and tell them that I had become a follower of Jesus. (I didn't even know the term "Christian" then.) My family and most of my friends just thought I was a little weird. My father didn't at all take me seriously.

In my seventh grade year my father's friend received Christ and began attending a local church. She invited my father to go to church with her. That is when I started attending church, hearing the Word of God and submitting to baptism. At first my father was trying to be open-minded about my newfound faith, but when I refused to bow down and worship at the altar of our ancestors, he became really angry. For my punishment I was forced to stay on my knees on the concrete floor in our apartment for two hours. I prayed for Jesus to make a way not to have to worship my ancestors. The next few times when my family was ready to offer incense to the ancestors, I would try to hide. When I was forced to kneel before the altar, I would pray that God would forgive me for kneeling down. Finally, my father gave up trying to force me to join them in worship. Jesus did make a way.

Several of my friends from the church youth group were beaten severely by their parents for coming to church and reading their Bibles. God spared me from the beatings, but my mother burned my first Bible that I received at my baptism. I bought a new Bible and hid it from my mother after that.

My father didn't allow me to go to church after I refused to worship the ancestors; he did, however, allow me to read my Bible at home. For two years I read the Bible at home and mailed my tithe to the church. In my tenth grade year the Holy Spirit started stirring my heart to ask my father for permission to go to church again, but I was afraid. I tried to convince myself that I could still be a Christian by reading my Bible at home. I even tried to find Bible study materials at a local Bible bookstore to prove to God that I could do this at home. For about three days I wrestled with the Holy Spirit. Finally on my way home from the Bible bookstore, Jesus asked me, "I suffered on the Cross for you. Why wouldn't you face your father for My sake?" When I arrived at home I asked my father for permission to go to church and instead of getting angry, he gave me his consent.

I started attending church regularly again and was excited about God, but my heart was still broken. My parents eventually got a divorce, my mother left us and my father passed away the summer before my senior year. There was no welfare system in Taiwan in 1990, and we didn't have any extended family members who would care for us. People at the church tried to be an aid when we were in need, but most of the time my sisters and I were all left on our own.

I managed to finish high school, even though I was at the edge of experiencing a nervous breakdown. I was so depressed I didn't want to get up in the mornings and I would dread to go to bed each night. There were nights that all I could do was rock myself in the bed as I cried hysterically. The only prayer I had was "JESUS," but that was enough. God reached out to me at the depth of my depression and the Holy Spirit baptized me in a dream; I woke up speaking in a new prayer language. Little by little, piece by piece God restored my heart and my emotions, but I was still not whole; there was still a missing piece.

After I came to America and started attending Living Word Church, I learned about the authority of the believer and deliverance from demonic spirits. As I submitted to the authority of loving and Godly deliverance ministers, I began to experience a new wholeness that I had never before experienced in my life. I have been set free from many generational curses and demonic forces. Many of my Taiwanese friends have also been set free from demonic spirits. During one Bible study, a Taiwanese girl could not confess and receive Jesus as Lord. The Bible study leader noticed that she had a jade pendant carved in the image of Buddha. We asked her to take the necklace off, and immediately, she was able to receive Jesus as her Lord and Savior.

Since the majority of Chinese values and beliefs are so intertwined with Buddhism and pagan religion, it is a big decision for one to choose to follow Jesus. After the birth of my first child, I came to a deeper realization of the impact of my Chinese background and how much more of my life and my beliefs I needed to give up to be conformed to what God wanted me to be. I realized that I could not tell my daughter the same bedtime stories my father once told me because they involved fairies and pagan gods; we could not celebrate Chinese holidays the ways in which my family celebrated when I was growing up. As a Chinese believer, I truly had to give up *who I was* to be *who I am* in Christ, and my children will never be able to fully embrace their Chinese heritage. Each day I have to choose to build the foundation of my children in the Word of God instead of in their inherited culture. For this I can imagine that the Lord asks me the same question as He did years ago, "I died and suffered for you on the cross. Would you give up what you had for My sake?" This time the answer is, "Gladly, my Lord!"

Author's comment: It does my heart good every time I see a Buddhist come to the Lord, after my failed, first attempt!

Rebekah and John Miller and Sunshine

Dear Peggy Joyce,

I wanted to take this opportunity to share the victory that I am enjoying because of my deliverance. I wish my family and church friends could understand how life changing deliverance is and how powerful and loving God is!

Please tell David and Angelia that I am 20 weeks pregnant (half way there) with our first child! And we are still heading for the mission field. You and your family have made a tremendous impact on me. I don't know where I'd be in life without all the truths that have been sown into my life. I really don't have words to describe the effect you and Dave and Angelia have had in opening my eyes to who God is, in helping me to seek a deep, intimate relationship with Him and in discovering the life changing power of deliverance.

In seventh grade I was diagnosed with narcolepsy, a sleeping disorder. My Spanish teacher, who was probably very tired of my sleeping through her classes and drooling on her tests, called my mother and told her that she thought I should be tested for narcolepsy. It didn't take long until I was taking prescriptions. It seemed that every six months or so the drug would quit working so my doctor would either increase my dosage or change me to another drug that would work great for the next six or eight months. My doctor told me that many people with this disorder fell asleep standing up.

When I turned 16 the question arose, "Can I drive?" I fell asleep in just about every car ride, even the one on the way to school which was less than five minutes every morning. I begged my doctor and assured him that on the medication I was fine, which was almost the truth. He wrote a letter for me and I had to appear before the court to get permission to have a driver's license. I only totaled three cars in high school. Fortunately, no one was severely injured and my parents had great insurance for me to cover the other cars that were involved.

I went through the first two years of college without a car. However, my junior year my parents decided to buy me one since I had moved into an apartment and needed a way to buy groceries, etc. I went to David and Angelia to ask if I could be healed from narcolepsy and what exactly would that mean. Could I stop taking the drugs that I had depended on for so many years? They took me through deliverance, but they did not tell me to stop taking all the drugs. Instead, they told me to get into the Word of God and pray for His direction. At this point I had several containers of prescription and over-the-counter wonders that I took daily—about eight in all. After my deliverance I quit taking all my prescriptions and only took multiple vitamins for the next year. I waited about six months before I made an appointment to tell the doctor I had quit taking the medicine, and needless to say, he was not very happy or convinced that I could make it without drugs. Even though I was diagnosed to have narcolepsy, by the blood of Jesus I am free from any effects of the disorder and I have to give God the credit for bringing me to the place of not having to be dependent on meds and doctors.

I am not going to say that I did not need power naps and an over-the-counter energy booster to get me through the next few years. Today, I thank God for continuing to help me and for delivering me from my dependence on prescriptions and a ton of fear that came along with it. I found that my diet was a big part of those triggers that zapped my energy and forced me to take a nap before continuing my task at hand. As long as I take a good vitamin and stay away from white sugar and refined flour, which aren't good for you anyway, I am as normal as, and probably healthier than, everyone else around me. I don't even need the energy booster that I once relied on. God is SO GOOD and the future looks brighter and brighter every day. His grace is more than sufficient for me!

Author's Note: So many people are asking for a healing when it is a deliverance they need. Just as in the case of the woman in Luke 13: 16, deliverance can often play a big part in physical healing when the problem is of demonic origin.

Deliverance from Homosexuality

Let me start off by stating one fact: God is good ALL the time. In my wildest dreams I never would have thought that I would be where I am today. Without God and His grace I would not be sitting here writing the account of my deliverance.

The appearance of my life just nine years ago was put together, on track and headed for nothing but greatness. Inside, however, I was in hopelessness and despair 24/7. I went to church. I had a prayer life. I had "accepted" Jesus as Savior. I had even gotten to the point in my life where I walked the Christian walk in public. I had *everything!* "God" was blessing me. But in reality, I was living how I wanted to live, with whomever I wanted to live and wherever I wanted to live. There was only *one* thing that made life miserable and unbearable. I was gay. This one area of my life was all that was keeping me from being happy. Now, looking back, this part of me ran deep and wide. It was a cancer that infected every aspect of my life and had me on the fast track to nowhere.

I grew up in a small town in New Mexico. A good thing about small towns is that you know everyone; a bad thing about small towns is that everyone knows you. I acquired the reputation of being "girly" very early in life. That eventually led to the "gay" label—which, in turn, led me into believing that I was destined for that lifestyle. I was molested at a late age (sixteen), and that was the event in my life that threw the door to homosexuality wide open.

I was raised primarily in a denominational church. I was extremely active—to the point of ridiculousness. I was in the building every time the doors were open. I was a leader in my youth group, active in the Church Council, a big player in worship, a Lay Leader, member of the Youth Praise Team, member of the youth choir, the adult choir, helper with children's choir, organizer for youth services and fundraisers... I WAS IN CHURCH. I couldn't understand that being active in church doesn't get one into heaven. I also held down a full, part-time job. I was a jack-of-all-trades. I was headed into the business world and was going to end up owning the biggest business around. God, however, had other plans.

In my sophomore year of High School my grandparents decided to move and had been trying to convince me that I needed to attend the university there in Dallas. My grandparents' decision to move there sort of clinched the deal. I would attend the University and then move to attend a larger University later to get the degree I desired. I would major in business with a minor in music and life would be good. So, as early as my sophomore year everything was lined up. My mind was made. I was accepted at both Universities and was offered healthy scholarships—but something inside told me that I needed to go to the one in Dallas first.

I went as a business major with a minor in music, but the day before classes started everything changed. (Keep in mind that I prayed and heard God; I was just living a completely detestable lifestyle.) I changed to my current major in the fall.

I knew that by going to a Christian University, I would have to keep my homosexuality under wraps, but I believed I could be "who I was" regardless. I had dated both guys and girls in high school, so I dated both guys and girls in college. That, however, over the course of a semester, changed to just guys. I knew that the life I was living wasn't right, but I didn't know how to change or where to go to even find out how to change. From my point of view the Bible didn't offer much help. It told me that homosexuals would not enter the kingdom of heaven (I Corinthians 6: 9), but it didn't tell me how to change. I was extremely embarrassed, so I didn't want to go to any pastor that I knew, and I certainly was not going to go to my parents. So life continued on in its destructive path until God started to change things.

In mid-November of that year I was diagnosed with rheumatoid arthritis. I firmly believe that this was an attack from Satan. He was trying to get me to despair and to return to my former major and get into a business where homosexuality is not "taboo" and is widely accepted. I also believe that if I hadn't accepted Christ at an early age, I would have taken that detour. Being a sophomore percussion major with juries around the corner, that diagnosis was certainly not good. My hands had doubled in size from swelling and were so stiff that it took one hand to close the other. For two months they were like that. It was impossible to practice except 30 minutes every four or five hours and that was not nearly enough to get me through the next semester. I needed help in a major way. My doctor even went so far as to tell me that I needed to consider changing my major. Again, God had different plans. In January

I had been invited to attend a local college Bible study, but forgot to go. I was so afraid that I had offended the girl who had invited me, mainly because I really liked her. I then reasoned that she could tell that I was gay, so what difference could it make if I offended her? I saw her the next day and apologized for not being there and she more or less blew me off. I promised that I would be there the next week, and I didn't go back on my word. I was there, and God had a plan for me that night.

A professor from a large university had stopped in to see the Bible study leaders. They were personal friends and they invited him to speak. Little did I know that this "speaking" would be in the form of *Word of Knowledge* and *Healing* (I Corinthians 12: 8-9). My flesh crawled and squirmed while this guy called out sore throats and achy body parts. All the while Satan was telling me, "This guy is a fake, a liar and a heretic." I wanted to leave. Then he called for "someone who was having problems with their hands." "He could have guessed that," I thought. So I waited and didn't say a word. Then he looked me in the eye and said, "You are having problems with your hands. The Lord wants to heal you. Come up here and let me pray for you." I just surmised that a little prayer never hurt anyone, and up I went. That night I was healed of arthritis and migraine headaches. I was supposed to be on Vioxx for the rest of my life, and I quit taking it the next day, along with my migraine medicine. My doctor tried to tell me that there must have been a misdiagnosis and that I really had tendonitis, or perhaps, bursitis, but not arthritis. I told him that God healed me and that was enough explanation for me. What really amazed me was that God healed me despite my unbelief. My faith in God grew leaps and bounds in that one evening.

I plugged myself into that Bible study group. I didn't really know anyone, and I didn't want anyone to **really** know me. I became more and more active with the group and started opening up to a couple of them. Two weeks after my deliverance from arthritis, the Bible study leader was giving me a Word of Knowledge and Prophecy. I prayed the whole time that God would not call me out on homosexuality in front of this group that had actually started to accept me for who I was, not for what I could do for them. God was faithful in granting that request. He told me that I would know God on a level that I could not fathom. He had me stretch my arms out—like I was about to give someone the biggest hug of my life—and then he said, "That doesn't even come close to the knowledge you will have about God." Immediately after Bible study that night a guy came up to me and told me that God told him to give me a "word."

That word was, "You are not!" That was all that was said, and it took every ounce of energy that I had not to bolt and bawl my eyes out. God had just answered my long prayed prayer. This guy told me that if I ever needed to talk I could call him—day or night, early or late. He gave me his home number, his work number and his e-mail address. Those went into my glove box and eventually disappeared. In my mind he was the one who had to make the next move. I was too proud to admit that God was right and that I was seriously wrong.

Finally God prompted this guy to call and invite me to dinner, gave me his testimony about homosexuality and his deliverance. He and I became very close and I could tell him ANYTHING, and I did—most of the time. Then in early March my life hit rock bottom.

The Lord had been working on me about some guys I was hanging out with and befriending. I thought I could help others who were dealing with this (WRONG!), so I decided that I would let this gay guy stay in my dorm room for the weekend. I didn't have a roommate, so I didn't have anyone else's space to consider. That night we ended up in bed together and the next morning I felt like a prostitute. I had no self worth and no light at the end of my tunnel. I pulled myself together and told him that we could be friends, but nothing more. He could call me, but I wasn't gay, so we had to keep it on a friend level. WRONG! He called me the next weekend, and I made it abundantly clear that we were just friends, but once again, I fell. I knew then that I could not handle this alone—that I had to find help and find it fast.

I went to my good friend first and he wasn't home. I then went to the Bible study leaders. It was Saturday and I was in desperate need of some help.

I didn't want to talk to a man; I wanted a woman to hear my story, so his wife and I sat down in their den and I spilled it all. I was gay and wanted out. I told her almost everything, leaving out only the specific details. She said that her husband was going to come in and ask me a few questions and then he was going to pray for me. I didn't want to tell this man of God what I was dealing with. I was embarrassed and ashamed of what I had done, but he came in and asked his questions— to which I gave short answers; and we went to prayer. That day will forever live in my memory as the day salvation came to my house. That was the day the Lord marked me for His own. That was the day I was set free from the bondage of sin and death. I was delivered from homosexuality, pornography, alcoholism, effeminacy, self-hate, self-destruction, and countless other cancerous things in my life. As I said before, homosexuality ran deep and wide and had infected every aspect of my life. It was much bigger than I could have ever imagined.

One common misconception about homosexuality is that it is small and can be turned off, but that is a lie. If you think you can turn it on and off, it is only because Satan lets you turn it on and off for a while to lull you into a false sense of security. Deliverance is not instantaneous. We live in a society of instant "this" and super fast "that." Deliverance is a process, much like life. Once you resist the enemy and take your initial stand on the Word, then you have to walk in your stand and not let your guard down. You have to walk in the grace of God daily, for without His grace you don't have life. Just this week He taught me another very important step—to release myself to God and fully trust Him **to cleanse my heart from my past.** What a marvelous difference that made. In that moment of time I entered into an even deeper dimension of His peace and joy than I had ever known before. The old has passed away and we are a new creation—take that all the way in your heart and clean out the mess. Receive the blessings the Lord desires for your life. He is ready to give them; all you have to do is accept them. It is your choice.

Corrie Ten Boom
Excerpt from *Tramp for the Lord*

When Corrie Ten Boom was holding a meeting in one of the Communist countries, she was disturbed that the people seemed helpless to receive. She said that they appeared to be like chained animals, dying of hunger, but unable to reach the food. It was as if the devil had a fence around the people so that they couldn't be reached. Finally Corrie realized that they were bound by demon powers. The next night she explained to the people that they were in bondage and then she proceeded to command all dark powers that were keeping the people from the blessings of God to go in Jesus' Name. After that she said that a miracle happened. The people who had been in bondage came alive. They began to rejoice and eagerly receive the message that was being presented to them. Corrie saw the tragedy of people, even men of God, who do not recognize that we are surrounded, not only by angels, but also by the powers of darkness. She would sadly say that missionaries have been given all, but not all missionaries have taken all of the boundless resources of God's promises, namely, the power of the blood of Jesus—and every Christian's legal right to use the wonderful Name of Jesus to cast out demons.

It has been said that when the existence of evil spirits is recognized by the heathen, it is generally looked upon by the missionary as 'superstition' and ignorance; whereas, the ignorance is often on the part of the missionary who is blinded by the prince of the power of the air to the revelation given in the Scriptures concerning the satanic powers.

She quoted C. S. Lewis as saying, *"There are two equal and opposite errors into which our race can fall about the devils. One is to disbelieve in their existence; the other is to believe and feel an unhealthy interest in them! They themselves are equally pleased by both errors, and they hail a materialist or a magician view with the same delight."*

Corrie say, "We have a good safeguard and guide—the Bible—God's Word. Here we find not only the necessary information about Satan and demons, but also the weapons and the armor that we need for this battle."

When Corrie and her sister Betsie had little to eat in the concentration camp at Ravensbruck, Betsie would dedicate the involuntary fast to the Lord so that it would turn to be a blessing. Almost immediately they said that they would then have power over the demons that were tormenting them, and they would be able to exercise that power to cast them out of their barrack. Their faith was in the fact that Mark 16: 17 says, "*In My Name those who believe will cast out demons.*" They said that they knew their fight was not against physical enemies, but against spiritual powers.

Corrie recalled one very significant incident that happened while they were ministering in Poland. She and her traveling companion, Conny, were becoming more exhausted the longer they stayed in Poland, but they didn't necessarily feel sick. One day they met an old friend from Holland and after describing the heaviness they felt, he asked if this was their first time to work in Poland. He then explained that the tiredness was nothing less than an attack of the devil because he did not like their work in that country since the antichrist was busy there arranging his army. The friend reminded them that whenever they experienced those attacks they must rebuke them in the Name of Jesus. They said that they learned a valuable lesson—that in a country where a godless philosophy reigns, only by claiming the blood of Jesus can you stand and not fall. Wherever Jesus Christ is not recognized as Supreme, then darkness rules and only by the authority in His Name can it be overcome.

WHAT MUST I DO TO BE SAVED?

The promises from God in this book are for God's children who love Him. If you have never given your life to Jesus and accepted Him as your Lord and Savior, there is no better time than right now.

There is none righteous, not even one.
-- Romans 3: 10

...for all have sinned and fallen short of the glory of God. *--Romans 3: 23*

God loves you and gave His life that you might live eternally with Him.

But God demonstrates His own love toward us, in that while we were yet sinners, Christ died for us.
--Romans 5: 8

For God so loved the world (you), that He gave His only begotten Son, that whoever believes in Him should not perish but have eternal life.
--John 3: 16

There is nothing we can do to earn our salvation or to make ourselves good enough to go to heaven. It is a free gift!

*For the wages of sin is death, but the free gift of
God is eternal life in Christ Jesus. --Romans 6: 23*

There is also no other avenue through which we can reach heaven, other than Jesus Christ—God's Son.

*And there is salvation in no one else; for there is
no other name under heaven that has been given
among men, by which we must be saved.*
--Acts 4:12

*Jesus said to him, "I am the way, and the Truth,
and the Life; no one comes to the Father, but
through Me."   --John 14: 6*

You must believe that Jesus is the Son of God, that He died on the cross for your sins, and that He rose again on the third day.

*...who (Jesus) was declared with power to be the
Son of God by the resurrection from the dead...*
--Romans 1: 4

You may be thinking, "How do I accept Jesus and become His child?" God in His Love has made it so easy.

*If you confess with your mouth the Lord Jesus
and believe in your heart that God raised Him
from the dead, you shall be saved. —Romans 10: 9
But as many as received Him, to them He gave
the right to become children of God, even to
those who believe in His Name.   --John 1: 12*

It is as simple as praying a prayer similar to this one—if you sincerely mean it in your heart:

Dear God:
    I confess that I am a sinner. I deserve to go to hell. But I believe that Jesus died for me, that He shed His Blood to pay for my sins and that You raised Him from the dead so that I can be Your child and live with You eternally in heaven. I am asking Jesus to come into my heart and save me. I confess Him right now as my lord.
    I thank You, dear Lord, for loving me and saving me. Take my life and use it for Your Glory.

                                    In Jesus Name,
                                    Amen

Help Your Child Overcome His Greatest Fears!

Would you like for your child to know how to overcome the fears that face him? Children in today's world are faced with so many more worries and uncertainties than those even a generation ago, but you are not without an answer. *Psalm 91 for Children* or *Psalm 91 for Youth* can be one of the greatest gifts you can give your child for equipping him to meet the challenge. Filled with heartwarming stories of young people who have stood on God's Word, this is a book that could very easily save his life and the lives of those he loves!

    Psalm 91 for Children and *Psalm 91 for Youth* are the identical book with different covers. The same format as the *Psalm 91 God's Umbrella of Protection* is used with the similar verse by verse look at God's Covenant of protection, but it's written on a reading level for young people and filled to overflowing with testimonies, illustrations, a picture album and application helps to make this truth come alive.

IS THERE A YEARNING IN YOUR HEART
TO TRUST GOD MORE?

Those Who Trust the Lord Shall Not Be Disappointed has the potential of building a trust in God like nothing you have ever read. Deep down, we direct our disappointments toward God—thinking that somehow He let us down. We trust God for our **eternal** life; why then can we not trust Him amid the adversities of **daily** life? Peggy Joyce Ruth has a unique way of showing that victorious living depends upon our unwavering trust in God. She demonstrates with scores of personal experiences just how faithful God really is and details how you can develop that kind of trust which will not disappoint.

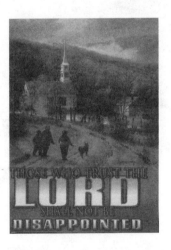

THOSE WHO TRUST IN THE LORD SHALL NOT BE DISAPPOINTED is a comprehensive study on developing a TRUST that cannot be shaken.

$8 plus $2 S& H.
Call 325 646 6894 or 1-877-97-books

To order additional copies with credit card call:
Phone: 325 646-6894
or Toll Free: (877) 97-BOOKS (877 972-6657)
or
send $10.00* each plus $2.00 shipping for 1 to 4 books**
to
The Peggy Joyce Ruth BETTER LIVING Ministries
P.O. Box 1549
Brownwood, TX, 76804-1549

*Texas residents, add 6.25% sales tax
**call 325 646-6894 for postage cost
when ordering 5 books or more

Impac **ian**
Chris **Books**

332 Leffingwell Ave., Suite 101
Kirkwood, MO 63122